WEIGHING IT UP

WEIGHING IT UP

ALI VALENZUELA

Hodder
Children's
Books

A division of Hachette Children's Books

A Catalogue record for this book is available from the British Library

ISBN 978 0 340 98840 4

Typeset in Caslon by Avon DataSet Ltd,
Bidford on Avon, Warwickshire

Printed and bound in Great Britain by
CPI Bookmarque, Croydon

The paper and board used in this paperback by Hodder Children's Books
are natural recyclable products made from wood grown in sustainable
forests. The manufacturing processes conform to the environmental
regulations of the country of origin.

Hodder Children's Books
a division of Hachette Children's Books
338 Euston Road
London NW1 3BH
An Hachette UK Company
www.hachette.co.uk

Contents

Introduction

Why I wrote this book

So often we hear of fad diets and the latest way to change our image to 'improve' ourselves. We see stick-thin celebrities and are bombarded with images of flawless women and gorgeous men. Realistically, this 'perception' that we are instructed to imitate is unattainable and my own horrific experiences have taught me that no matter how much you try to manipulate yourself to feel accepted, you must accept yourself and love yourself before others can do the same.

The following extracts are from the diaries I kept while battling with anorexia:

I want people to understand that there is more to anorexia than looking thin; this is an illness that will destroy the lives of the sufferer and all who care for the sufferer and the thin appearance is only a physical outcome of the pain and torment that goes on inside.

I feel open to talking about my experience, as it may help other people. Just because I went through a difficult struggle doesn't mean that something positive cannot come of it.

I wrote this in the gap year that I was forced to take because my anorexia was too severe for me to go to university. It is the year that I came out of hospital, and decided to use the illness in any possible way that I could. It sums up my main motivation for writing this book. Just because I have had a negative experience of anorexia it doesn't mean I can't create a positive outcome for someone else. If one sufferer feels less alone by reading about my experience, or if a carer of an anorexic sufferer feels they can understand the illness better, that to me is a positive outcome.

And even I can take some positive things from my experience. Despite the immense suffering, both mental and physical, that I went through at the time, I feel it was something that made me who I am today: a strong, determined person who has learned the importance of self-respect, and is capable of escaping death through sheer determination to live a wonderfully fulfilling life. I now know my weaknesses and can develop my strengths to persevere through anything that life may throw at me.

About Me

I was born and grew up in Swansea, South Wales, in a loving, caring family. As my father is Chilean, we occasionally visited our family in Chile, yet normally spent our summer holidays in France, or just enjoying time together. Raised as a Catholic, I attended a Roman Catholic nursery and primary school, where I made many close friends who often came round to play.

Our house was always alive and welcoming. I have an older brother, Kevin, an older sister, Isabella, a nephew, Tom, and his mother, Toula, who was also a great part of my life. Although I was often surrounded with friendly faces, I was also happy to spend time on my own, entertaining myself by being creative or with music. With two lovely gardens, a relatively ample house, a nephew who was like a brother to me, and the park and beach very near to my house, my creative and imaginative mind was never deprived of activities. I loved music, and played the piano from the age of six. I loved animals, and had a pet dog and rabbit, and I enjoyed walking my dog along the beach.

From a family that loved food, particularly influenced by the Latino side of the family, delicious home meals were always prepared and there was never a shortage of food in the cupboards. Apart from my mother's strong intolerance to gluten, there were no issues around food; meals were simply an enjoyable opportunity to get together and socialize with those we loved the most.

Obsession and control

I visualize the illness as a growth or deformity that lives in the last vertebra of my spine. It's rotting and disgusting, like cancer that has grown over time and has stopped me doing all the things that I love to do. Physically, it is only small in size, but it has taken over my world and engulfed me.

If I need reassurance from it, I can feel it physically in my body and am flooded with a sense of relief by touching the bones. I'm terrified of the thought of not having the physical presence which makes people aware there is a problem because I know it will still be there even if it's not apparent to others.

Over time, I began to realize that this illness was not to do with reaching a certain weight, but with trying to live on air, with pushing myself when others rested, with starving when others ate. I was a battery-charged girl, no need of the necessities of food and rest.

With such a high focus in society today on diets, losing weight and shaping up, it is difficult not to get brainwashed and very tempting to excuse yourself from a meal just because a friend skipped lunch, or someone else isn't eating.

Personally, I never aspired to imitate the severe thinness of models, but I did aspire to be accepted, and irrationally believed that being thinner would make me 'fit in' more.

Chapter 1
The Start of It

There was no set point as to when the anorexia started; it just seemed to creep into my life.

Who would have thought it? After growing up in a loving family that had a healthy attitude to food and regularly enjoyed nutritious, home-cooked meals, an eating disorder was the last thing anyone expected of me.

My first sight of the dark and cruel world of anorexia was when I was about fourteen years old. I was suddenly rejected by my group of friends, and being sensitive, this rejection was a blow to my self confidence. I passed my long, lonely summer doing what made me feel good, what passed the time well and didn't require any company – I exercised.

It's such an insidious illness that it tricks the sufferer into believing that they are in control, even when it is clearly obvious to onlookers that they are not. The sufferer's own friends and family, the people who know them best, become frustrated and feel distant from this strange being, who looks like the person that they know and love, but is turning into a self-destructive stranger. The shocking weight loss, the secretive and disturbing eating habits, the obsessive nature towards all aspects of food, all are the effects of anorexia.

How it started

June 2003: age fourteen

I feel like I'm putting on a lot of weight at the moment so I'm on a diet and trying to do a lot of exercise (going to the gym tomorrow, walking home and sports day on Thursday! so should be all right). Avoiding sweets and shit too.

December 2003

I woke up really late (11.40) but was in the gym at 12.30! Was in there yesterday too; lots of exercise! I ate a Weetabix, a banana with cream, and chicken and potato, and now I weigh 8st 12! Pretty chuffed – I bought a tiny white skirt in town the other day and I want to look thin in it; hoping to get to 8st 7 by Xmas.

January 2004

I've been pretty good this week; went to the gym Tues, Thurs, Fri, on Wed I had dance class, had two hours' dance class today, and Sat night I danced all night until 12.30!

March 2004: age fifteen

ATM I'm on a diet – feel really fat lately and I have to get to 8st 6 (1lb loss). Increase exercise and decrease food – will be good about it though. No exercise makes me feel so frustrated.

September 2004

Weighing just under 8st and am 5 foot 7. Have been a bit lazy this summer, better get off my fat arse and do something! Periods have been gone for about four months.

Walking, swimming, gym – whatever, I did it. I also gained a sense of power by controlling my diet, and this lethal cocktail allowed me to lose weight. People began to compliment me on my weight loss, but that soon became comments of concern that I'd lost 'a bit too much weight'.

Weight issue getting kind of serious – form tutor told my head of year who told the nurse who phoned my mum (!).

She is 'concerned about the amount of weight I've recently lost' and she's been asking my friends if I'm bulimic and stuff! Sneaky cow, fair enough if she's concerned but there's no need to go behind my back. I will talk to her tomorrow and say 'thanks for your concern, but I'm fine'. Because I really don't know how or why I've lost so much. I DO NOT make myself sick! And I might be a bit obsessed about my weight and diet but it really isn't such a big thing. Anyway, me and Mum are going to the doctor's after school to see about my periods (haven't had any for six months), fainting and bowel problems etc. I guess I do want to go, to make sure I'm OK and everything, and I do know deep down that I should really put on a few more pounds. So I guess I ought to start soon, but I'm not breaking my New Year's resolution not to eat chocolate.

My concerned mother took me to my GP, who warned me that I was borderline anorexic. With the combined threat of having to see a psychiatrist, and of having my medical history revealing my bout with anorexia, I managed to gain weight with the doctor's advice on how to balance my diet with my extreme exercise levels, and steadily increased from 7st 7 to a healthier 9st 5.

October 2004

Apparently I'm on the verge of an eating disorder. I don't know what to say about it – I guess it's just one of those things and I count myself lucky that I have people around me who care about me and didn't let me get too bad. Weighing 7st 10lb-ish. Don't want people to worry though.

November 2004

Went to the doctor's – put on 1kg = ( ) and have to put on 2.5kg (5.5 pounds) in a month. Am referred to a dietician and have been told to eat: cereal and toast in the morning, midmorning snack, a whole sandwich for lunch, snack when I get home and carbs in my dinner. It will be a bitch but I will try.

2005

January 2005

I am eating enough for a small country, I just can't stop. Not only do I take whale-sized portions, I also can't control myself or monitor when I'm full, so I snack until I'm almost sick and can't bend down because my stomach feels and looks pregnant – ten months I swear! At least it's mainly healthy stuff, but I feel guilty for going on eating and yet I know I'm slim . . . OK, thin . . . Deep down I KNOW, it's just hard to explain what I am feeling.

February 2005: age sixteen

GOT MY PERIODS BACK! After almost one year without a period, I've finally gotten back up to a healthy weight – this is the sign from my body that I'm all in working order and am back on track! Yay – so chuffed!

All my family were relieved to see the weight go back on, and assumed that this had been a random phase simply due to stress over my GCSE examinations, and a change of friendship group.

However, looking back on my teenage diaries, I can see that I was focusing on fitting in by changing myself, because of my insecurity and self doubt.

Last night, all the girls were with a boy and I was ashamed as I was on my own practically all night – what the hell is wrong with me?! I feel like such a loser!

I have always had a great relationship with my parents, being far younger than my brother and sister made me close to my mother and father. (As a baby I was even mistaken for my sister's daughter.) My sister and I had always had a great relationship, too, and I loved going to visit the older sis up in London to do fun things like go shopping or go and watch All Saints live! When she married her partner – who I'm also close to

– they moved to Spain for his work, and during this time my illness may not have been physically apparent, but I still overheard her complaining to my parents about how I was 'still f—g anorexic' and it was 'driving' her 'crazy'.

May 2005 (mid GCSE exams)

Been really stressed lately, I think my anorexic mind is upon me as I've lost weight (now 52kg/8st 3). I have to put it on in two weeks for another doctor's appointment, or else she's referring me to a shrink! That would go on my record and I don't want that, although I sometimes think it might do me good . . . I'm just not interested in food now, even when I'm hungry! And now I have to put on weight, I don't know what to do. I love food but I've messed everything up. I want to be well but it's hard to overcome.

16th September 2005

Am a bit sad at the moment – I need to do more exercise, I want someone to fancy me and for me to like them back, I want to have no homework or hassle from that area. I can't stop thinking about food.

Not only had I become obsessive about exercise, but little rules began to filter in, and dictate how I always could have done better; how my attempts were never good enough.

Today I ate one Weetabix, popcorn chicken, a McFlurry and chicken and potato, a reasonable amount but I should've skipped lunch and the McFlurry, and only had one piece of chicken for dinner!

Despite the weight gain – that I knew was healthy – the rules and self hate continued inside, and the illness only lay dormant, yet never stopped reminding me of how I was unacceptable.

That year, after my GCSEs, I decided to move from my comprehensive school to college, despite the fact that only one other friend of mine was going there too. However, I enjoyed the opportunity to meet new people and to have a fresh start. I made lots of new friends, and finally met a guy that liked me as much as I liked him. We became great friends, and our relationship developed further.

People who had known me when I lost a lot of weight complimented me on how much better I looked, and my boyfriend often admired my curvy figure. But I remember the absolute panic I experienced as the scales read 9st 5lb. All I could think was how the weight

HAD to go, I HAD to shape up; if people realized what a sloppy mess I had become, surely they'd reject me again? Maybe they just said they liked me looking so fat so they looked better next to me?

I became absorbed in a punishing exercise regime, and became anxious, uptight and irritated if I couldn't do it. Over time, I preferred to exercise alone because other people would delay me and shorten the amount of time available for me to burn off all my horrendous flab.

Although I never went on pro-anorexia websites, I inspired my eating disorder with my own hand, writing a letter to myself to encourage me to keep up my self-destructive behaviour. Looking back and reading over it, it terrifies me to see how desperate I was to change myself and even how consumed I was by the anorexia, even when the weight loss at this point was not obvious. Before it became physically evident, this twisted illness totally consumed my mind.

2006

Letter to myself

Honestly don't eat anything because once you start you'll forget about your guilt and eat loads and after, when you've stuffed yourself, you'll remember your guilt and think of thin people like Eva and feel sad and promise yourself to go on a diet but you never do and now you're not thin, just normal, and if you carry on like this you'll be tubby, then plump, then chubby etc; not attractive!

You only have a few lb to lose, by the end of the week 9st is just so easy just keep telling yourself you're not hungry, you have no appetite. You've been eating too much lately and you have been so lazy – eww!

You'll look so much better just a little thinner; keep yourself from getting any bigger. People compliment your figure now for the same reasons you used to compliment people who'd put on weight. No-one likes to be the biggest!

If you're ABSOLUTELY starving (8 hours since last meal) have a diet fizzy drink/half a litre of water/cup of tea. Control yourself. Just imagine your potential discomfort. Fat is unacceptable. If you concentrate on studies and busy yourself, you'll be fine.

Rules

When it came to eating, I was swamped with rules. Firstly, there was the divide between the foods that I couldn't eat, like deep fried things, high calorie or fatty things, and the things that I was allowed, such as fruit or no-fat yoghurt. To make things more complicated, if I were to indulge in something enjoyable at some point, I would have to know in advance so that I could not only do a major workout, but also so that I could starve myself throughout the day, say for example if I were to go out for a meal later that evening. If I had to eat something, I had to really enjoy it, otherwise this would be a waste of calories, and if I ate something that I didn't enjoy I would feel so guilty and angry with myself that I'd have to spend the next day compensating for the wasted calories.

This led to me being irritable and anti-social during mealtimes, angry at those who distracted me from eating or appeared to pay attention to my eating, as I wanted to devote all my attention to the meal.

I feel very irritated when people try and talk to me when I'm trying to eat, as it distracts me and I don't like talking with my mouth full.

Anorexia gives you a set of rules that you simply must follow, and breaking out of these rules is not only extremely anxiety-provoking, but often sends you into a tremendous panic that often results in the illness taking over again. In fact, some rules were so detailed that it became almost impossible to match the specific demands made by the illness.

If I identify my behaviour as anorexic, I feel stronger. My anorexia makes me feel good about not eating so much fat – I become less of a pig, and it's an excuse to myself (I may have had 600kcal, but 0g fat!).

For others, these rules do not apply. For example, if they eat a slice of cake, it won't matter. But if you were to eat even half a slice, not only would everyone be shocked at what a pig you are, but you would get out of control, not be able to stop eating and it would really show on you. You would prove how out of control you really are if you were to eat the cake.

I often felt that people had 'anorexic expectations' of me: that it would be so out of character of me to eat say, a slice of cake, or a normal portion of the evening meal. I also became so ashamed if I were to help myself to something 'out of the rules' that if someone were to comment, I would become so angry that my cheating ways had been noticed, I wouldn't be able to eat it, and would throw it away to prove I hadn't eaten it.

Chapter Two

Letter From a Friend

The illness began infiltrating me completely; my life began to change in more ways than just my eating habits. My daily routine was structured around college, tearing off for sneaky gym sessions as often as possible, and earning money several nights a week in a restaurant. In Summer 2006 I went on a wonderful holiday in Germany with my boyfriend, followed almost instantly by a two-week stay with my sister in Spain. On my return after almost a month of eating hardly much more than fruit and the occasional meal, my friends were shocked at my transformation. Going into the second year of college was now completely different; I couldn't deny I was infected with an insidious illness that was slowly but surely taking over my life. Routine visits to the doctor began again in August.

The illness panics when others begin to detect its presence: thus it makes the sufferer react angrily and defensively.

The illness makes you secretive and irritated by the concern of others, wanting to get on with breaking you down without being interrupted. Thus, it is very difficult to get the sufferer of an eating disorder to admit there is something wrong.

It's confusing living in this world in my head – this crazy world of famine and self control forces me to obsess and dream over forbidden foods, then punish myself with guilty thoughts of how any morsel of food that passed my lips has made me a failure.

It's no longer a deprivation to avoid getting fatter; it's a game of power, between me and some strange competitive force inside of me. Of strength and power, of coping without the basic necessities for every human being, of pushing past the norm and relying solely on myself.

My energy isn't from my food consumption (how could it be?!) but from this frustration and anger which every now and then bubbles up inside, giving me the willpower to keep going.

Let me survive without food, and be perceived as having amazing willpower.

Let me see all those who try and feed me as interference to becoming my greater self.

Let me convert all signs of warning and disapproval from others into encouragement that I'm succeeding in my game of power.

But why?! I'm so afraid of drifting away in this world of mine, where even the closest of friends are strangers, maybe even drifting away from my own self. People don't understand me – how can they when I don't even understand myself?!

Why is there constantly food on my mind, even when my friends talk about boys, or clothes, or work? I honestly can't think of anything more exciting than fantasizing over delicious foods!

I've got to a point where I find myself disliking things purely because they're calorific or fattening, even when I know I have loved them! Sometimes I eat something I 'shouldn't', and this unexplainable explosion of anger erupts inside me; my eyes are wide and my brain is screaming for me to stop – stop you greedy bitch!

There's no control left, no appealing to my brain. I've lost the game. I know I look shit, desperately cramming food into my mouth like an animal that hasn't eaten for days. But my anger is so strong, I hate myself for losing control and being a failure, I hate whoever is with me for watching me commit that disgusting deed (how humiliating) and how can they allow me to continue?!

When I dream of food it rarely touches my lips; I dream of larger than life versions of things I can destroy, jump on, roll in, squash with my fingers and mash with my feet – into a horrible lumpy mess, repellent to eat. Now, I don't even have to touch it for it to be repulsive! My mind does that for me. When I lose my appetite, as normal people sometimes do from time to time, I want to eat but nothing will suffice, but if I eat when I'm not hungry, I'm failing myself. How can I win?!

I hate food – this hate has become an obsession; I am obsessed with food so relish every opportunity to touch, feel, smell, talk or think about food, as long as I DO NOT EAT IT; the one thing it was meant for.

I'm so confused yet this weird anxiety over food has formed into a safety net to stop me becoming fat and unattractive. I'm safe from being ugly by being insane! I disgust myself with my crazy obsession, but I feel safe, secure. And I know deep down, this is no longer just a safety net to catch me, but it has turned on me, and is now dragging me down. And I can't escape.

Over time, I began to realize that this illness was not to do with reaching a certain weight, but with achieving living on air, with pushing myself when others rested, with starving when others ate. I was a battery-charged girl, with no need for the simplest things such as food and rest.

Letter from my friend

One of my best friends, who stuck by me throughout my illness and is still a very important person in my life, wrote me a letter explaining how she felt I was getting ill again.

Dear Alikins,

Recently me and your close friends have noticed that you seem to be slipping into your old eating habits again. This is a letter from only me and I wanted to write it, instead of confronting you about these things because I know it's a sensitive topic with you, but I want you to know I'm writing this not to offend you or blowing things out of proportion, but because I don't want you to harm yourself like you did before. You probably feel like you are not doing anything wrong, but even though you know what you are doing you are blind to the physical consequences and effects.

You think you have to lose weight and I think forever

there will always be that in the back of your mind. You are probably thinking that I'm just on your back like everyone else, but you have to understand that obviously there is something wrong if so many people mention it. When people say things like 'Ali, you're looking too thin' it makes you feel good. Even though you know that this is a sign of an eating disorder. You might be content with this and continue to do it, and if you keep doing it, it'll never go away, you have to think of the last time you were ill and all the physical effects of what you'd done to your body. But in my eyes, the psychological ones are much worse. I know you don't like to hear this, and just think that me and a lot of people just exaggerate, why can't we leave you to it? The way you are at the moment, you are not suffering in any way but you could get seriously ill, and I think that's a very likely reality for you, Ali. You have to think of whether you want to be tormented by your thoughts of never being good enough forever.

Ali, you are beautiful and it annoys and frustrates me that you can't see it, and I think this is about the millionth time I've said this but you do not, 1000%, need to lose a single pound. In everyone's opinion if anything, you need to put on weight. But I never know whether giving you compliments is a good idea, because I know that it spurs you on further to lose weight. You need to realize skinny does not = beauty, skinny does not = attractive.

Sometimes I just feel like shaking you and telling you to stop it but the way you think about this means that you don't listen to me, Al. I think you are even in denial that you have a problem. I just want you to stop now, Ali. I know that you need to realize these things yourself but I can't stand watching you starve yourself and do excessive amounts of exercise, I just want you to sort it now so that you can get better and so that this doesn't keep coming back again and again, even though it's the kind of thing you will always have in some way. I just don't want it to affect you, and your health in such a way in the future.

We care about you Ali, please realize that what you do isn't right, just try and take in what I've said. You know I'm right.

Love you Al xxxxx

I was so angry after receiving this letter, and felt like all the people closest to me had been ganging up behind my back to gossip about my secret and shameful obsession. I refused to agree with her, and wrote an aggressive letter back. Yet her words remained in my head, and after a confirmation by my GP, I had to admit that I had anorexia.

Looking back, I can see her concern and desperation to see a glimpse into the anorexic pit I was falling deeper and deeper into, but even at the point when my illness wasn't physically obvious, I was mentally in a completely alien world.

September 2006

I went to the doctor's today and she told me that I had gotten to a point of anorexia where she could no longer help me and the only thing she could do is to speed up my referral to a psychiatrist. I am relieved I'm going to get this help but I don't want to be hospitalized and I don't want to feel alone and confused like I do. I know I need to change and when I saw 7st on the scales I realized how trapped I am because despite wanting to be healthy, I'm stuck in this deluded sense of control. My friends walk on eggshells around me, and my parents are worried sick; no one is the same with me. Yet, I still carry on, letting myself suffer to such an extent that it is starting to affect those around me. Like the barrel of suffering inside me has burst and now is leaking out on to those close to me. I love life too much to be overcome by this illness, but one step at a time . . . things change without me even knowing. I'm terrified of isolation, so why am I putting myself through it? I'm so full of misunderstanding, I can't begin to think.

I would constantly need to justify eating anything. Eating was only OK when I had saved or restricted myself beforehand.

Friday 22nd September 2006

Sugar free jelly with low fat custard – 8.30am in kitchen alone. Would rather not have had custard but it's OK as I know it's low fat.

Chicken and red pepper wrap – 6.45pm in work alone. Felt fine as I've saved myself for it and enjoyed it.

Exercise: 800kcal in gym, 400 situps, 150 arm weights (5lb).

October 2006

My anorexia is winning. I feel so down all the time that I feel like crying constantly, and I feel so alone that my appetite is non-existent; the last thing I want to do is eat, and feel those horrible feelings of self disgust and frustration and guilt on top of how shit I feel right now.

I'm so scared that my studies are going to suffer and yet I'm still going to the gym four times a week for exhausting sessions, and controlling my eating etc.

I never see the girls any more – we all have lots of work. At least I think that's the reason . . .

Me and my boyfriend have split up because I'm not giving him the attention he needs – I just cannot give him the relationship he wants, I don't have the energy!

I can't be bothered for a lot of things.

However, I passed my driving test not long ago so I'm a lot more independent, and I'm going to a psychiatrist every week. So far I'm keeping a food diary including feelings, where, when and who I'm with when I eat. I had a big pig-out today – so much cheese, and peanut butter, and Nutella.

Feeling full makes me panic and want to starve, but I know I can fight this, even when I feel alone. My parents are very much here for me at the moment, but it's hard for them too.

Despite having common sense and intelligence, I was unable to recognize the effects of extreme starvation in myself.

December 2006

I am going to fight anorexia. I have been to one of my psychiatrist appointments, weighed in at 41.3kg (6st 7) today and have overheard my parents talking to their friend who is convinced I should be sent to The Priory, a clinic for eating disorders in Bristol, or to the nearby hospital for nasogastric feeding.

Mum came to my shrink session today, has replayed everything to my dad and her friend, so I feel angry at her for not respecting my privacy, but then she is the only one who has faith in me, who believes that I can get better at home, which I love her for.

If I continue, will my relationship with my dad

deteriorate? In fact, will I just die? It's not a reality to me, but it's the only thing for me if I carry on.

Why, at such an important time of my life, should it take over with such disastrous effects? Am I just stupid, enjoying the security of being locked in a false sense of control? I know people are talking about me, so my paranoia is just confirmed when I overhear conversations like the one between my parents and their friend. Is it paranoia when it's really happening, or just being aware?!

Chapter Three

Hospital

Things really started to get serious in 2007.

Despite visiting my psychiatrist twice a week for a weigh-in and a chat to him, this hadn't prevented the anorexia from growing and developing, consuming me in the process. I was prescribed high calorie supplement drinks, which occasionally I tried to knock back when I was desperate to fight the illness. But guilt would swarm over me, and I wanted to at least enjoy taking in the calories if I had to put on weight, so the majority of the drinks ended up being poured down the sink.

My psychiatrist told me and my mum that once I hit the 40kg (6st 4) mark, I would be referred to The Priory Hospital. I brushed this off as hospitalization seemed to be for really ill people, not for me.

In my anorexic bubble, all that existed was food, and

I was absolutely obsessed. I would fantasize about it all day, surfing the internet, studying different types of foods and recipes around the world, even to the extent of making my own detailed cookbook full of the most rich, luxurious dishes that I would have loved to eat but didn't dare. Anything to do with food would catch my interest – looking back now, the only way that I remember certain occasions that happened during my illness is if someone reminds me of what we ate at that time!

Between manic workouts at the gym, working at a Mexican restaurant, revising for hours for my A Level exams, and obsessing about food, I had no time for anyone or anything else, including myself. It made me sick to be so obsessed; I was exhausted and ashamed with my painfully obvious obsession. The irony of it was that I only wanted what I couldn't have.

Once or twice I arranged a grand meal and invited all of my friends round. This gave me the opportunity to design a menu, fantasize over how to create delicious dishes, go shopping and buy all of the foods that I really loved, cook for hours in the kitchen, then see people devour the goods whilst I 'practised' my control, simply watching them enjoy.

(Now I enjoy cooking occasionally, but have made a rule for myself that if I am preparing something, I should participate in the eating, and I find this sociable act is a lot more enjoyable.)

I was still going to the gym, still going to college and studying for A levels, still going to work in the Mexican restaurant several times a week. Yet my boss started to notice my deterioration, and took me to the side one day, concerned that my sparkle had gone and my performance was worsening. As an effect, the number of shifts I was given dwindled. Every time I'd come back from a weigh-in session, my parents would look at me in desperate hope that I'd bring back the good news of weight gain, but their hope would be taken over by disappointment as I reported weight loss. I hated making them suffer so much, and would even assemble dishes to make out that I'd already eaten, in attempt to lessen their concern. However, this only made it impossible for them to trust their daughter who was so controlled by her illness to the extent of dishonesty.

Despite always being very close to my father, his inability to understand my illness simply frustrated him, and his helplessness infuriated him. He became subdued and I felt he avoided me, preferring to block out his pain by having a drink. I could sense when things were hard for him not by his words to me, but by hearing the chink of bottles as he reached for his relief.

This illness has definitely alerted me to how

important it is to communicate with one another, and discuss how you're feeling. Keeping it blocked up inside will only build up negative feelings.

I knew full well that this illness was destroying me, slowly peeling *me* down into nothingness, to grow itself. This is a letter of encouragement that I wrote myself.

I want to be without my anorexia. I love the person I am when I'm in full control of myself, and I do not want anyone else to have power over me when It harms me.

I am capable of three As at A level ONLY WITHOUT ANOREXIA

I am friendly, sociable and relaxed WITHOUT ANOREXIA

I have a spark that my anorexia has stolen

I want to exercise

I want to eat without people watching

I want to walk out of a room without worrying that people talk about me (paranoia)

I want to concentrate and focus

I want my passion for life back

I want more to life than suffering in myself – no more isolation or depression

I want to chat to my dad without seeing desperation and sadness in his eyes

I don't need excuses for failure – I'm not failing

I want to be free from anorexia, not a slave to it
I have false control but I want real control; all control will
be lost in hospital
I want to be stylish and fashionable

Anorexia has taken
– my capability
– beauty
– concentration
– passion
– freedom
– control
– parents' trust
– boyfriend
– style
– health

Running away

After yet another report of weight loss, the illness pushed my parents too far. They couldn't look at me, this strange being that had incorporated itself into their baby girl, and barely spoke to me.

I had had enough; enough of being regarded only for my illness, enough of feeling alone, enough of feeling guilty for putting my parents through so much suffering.

I decided that my presence in my home was causing more harm than good, so without another word, I left for college with a slightly bigger bag than normal, and didn't return.

I camped out at various friends' houses in the evenings, and spent the days in college.

That week I had a weigh-in, and came out of my doctor's in tears of frustration; I had lost weight once again and couldn't possibly tell my parents. I texted my sister-in-law to tell her I was so sorry and I couldn't tell my own parents how much I weighed, could she do it for me?

She told me how worried my mum was, how much she wanted me back, but I didn't want to be the cause of her suffering any more. I completely refused to go back home, but agreed a quick meet-up in Tesco with my mum, on neutral ground.

Mum came rushing towards me, buying me a bunch of flowers and a packet of grapes; for some reason the only thing I could eat in abundance was grapes! But the look in her face said it all to me. She loved me and wanted me back, and was not prepared to lose her daughter to an illness. Yes, it was hard, but a fight that was worth sticking through.

A few days later I came back home, and the approach was different. It was like we had a fresh start and although I'd lost weight, it didn't have to be this way for ever.

Everyone understands that the person with the illness suffers huge amounts, but you can't forget those around you, who suffer too. To this day I feel terrible for the nightmare I pulled my parents into, for the scraggly mess my friends had to hang around with.

It didn't just consume me, but it brought those around me into the same pit of despair.

Where am I, trapped alone in a world no one knows, no one understands. I want to get out and feel, but how can I when I have no path, no feelings inside of me? I'm an empty shell with a hollow heart and a hated body. No matter my size, or where I am in life, I will look at myself in disgust as I can never live up to my own expectations.

People tell me to aim for the sky, but how can I when I can't even look up?

You want the truth? NO, I AM NOT FUCKING ALL RIGHT!

I hate this body that I live in, this person that can never fulfil my expectations and needs to use an illness as an excuse so that others don't see the true failure that I am. I wouldn't want my worst enemy to feel what I feel right now. I want to escape from here, from the self-loathing and discomfort and disappointment.

July 2007

In hospital

I felt resigned to going to The Priory; that morning I had my crack-of-dawn walk along the seafront which involved sliding out of bed and into my walking shoes, creeping down the stairs so as not to wake anyone, and slipping out of the door. That was something my anorexia made me stick to; not having my daily walk was completely unacceptable. Sometimes, I would even walk down to town to wander the streets aimlessly, just so I could get an extra hour's exercise.

Mum drove me up to The Priory in Bristol, and although I wasn't sure what to expect and was unaware of any of the rules, I felt a small sense of relief that finally, control would be taken from me, and I had an excuse to escape from the anorexic lifestyle that I had been screaming to get out of for so long. It's like a child who is bullied reaching the teachers' staff room, to know that they are safe but also knowing that to admit what has been happening to them will be very scary, perhaps not even worth it.

The reception was luxurious and welcoming, and as I sat on a guest chair, clutching my suitcase, I was greeted by a nurse who came to meet me from the eating disorder unit. She walked me and Mum to 'my' room, and began the ritual bag search. Every single item I owned was taken out and noted down; potential tools for self-harm such as my nail file or tweezers were taken from me and locked away in the weigh-in room, along with the snacks, documents and medicines of the eating disorder unit.

In this room I was told to strip down to my underwear and turn away from the scales as the nurses recorded my weight and height, both numbers that I was forbidden to know. Yet from the shock on the nurse's face alone, I could tell it wasn't good news.

Next, I underwent a medical examination, a consultation with my consultant, and an explanation of the eating regulations and times. It was 12.30 and lucky me, I had arrived in time for lunch! So we trawled downstairs and I sat with several other patients on one out of three tables. The atmosphere was gloomy and miserable, and nobody wanted to be there. I had opted for a cheese and pickle sandwich (the dreaded carbohydrates had to be put in at some point!) and was shocked when I saw the measly quarter of a sandwich that was put in front of me.

It's so undermining being stripped of control and being treated with all of these rules really frustrates me. For example, all of my clothes and items were searched through, and items like my chewing gum and fizzy drink were confiscated.

I found it difficult the first few days not knowing any of the rules, learning them the hard way by stepping out of line and then being told how things were done there, and I felt like an outsider as I wanted to get better as quickly and efficiently as possible, which didn't seem to me to match with my feelings of hunger. I explained and complained to the nurses about how I wanted to increase my portion size, and when I did eventually talk to the dietician, felt slightly panicked and unsure that I could manage this increase.

I felt very passive coming into The Priory. My consultant seems calm yet uncompromising, and when she told me I would need a wheelchair and a stair lift to get around because I was in such an emaciated state, I burst into tears.

I have to stay in the lounge (like our common room) between 9 in the morning and 9.30 at night so that a nurse can watch what I'm up to; even in the night they come in every half an hour to check I'm not up to mischief, exercising in my room or something.

   My bathroom is locked in case I try and make myself

sick, and I have to ask one of the nurses to unlock it every time I need it; very humiliating. I even have to be supervised in the shower in case I faint!

I feel so down and afraid being in this strange, rule-consumed environment, but at the same time I feel I positively want to embrace my chance to get better; now that I'm here I may as well make the most of it – at £700 a night it's not exactly cheap!

During the first few weeks of being in hospital, I got on very well with the medical doctor that dealt with my physical problems, but a lot of the time he ended up helping me through tough mental times, too. When I felt the world was against me, and I was unsure about what I could do without breaking the rules, he assured me that I was making positive progress, and really made me feel special – for example, he told me that I was the only patient he had seen who had wanted more food! This reminded me of how much I wanted to get better, and that I was here only for me – the opinions of the other patients meant absolutely nothing. I was here for me, and not for them.

10th July 2007
I've started to realize that recovery is a lot more about the mental goings-on than simply putting on weight. I had a

chat to the doctor who helped me to see that horrible side effects of refeeding – like oedema [swelling of my body tissues] – will eventually lead to a fantastic life without anorexia, so it is my next goal to achieve!

He also said that I will get a belly, later that will disperse over my hips and although it may be uncomfortable and unfamiliar, I will become more settled in my mind and by identifying other benefits that I didn't have in an anorexic world, I can accept my body and become a more satisfied person in general.

I've noticed that around mealtimes I feel hot and flushed in my cheeks, my heart races and my hands shake uncontrollably, but according to the doctor this is just anxiety.

Nurses

Particularly during the first few weeks in which I was learning all the new rules, the nurses would keep a watchful eye on my eating habits and any attempts to lessen my intake. There was not a moment that I had to myself without a nurse checking up on me; every mouthful, every step around the lounge, every trip to the bathroom, a nurse would be there watching me, ensuring that my anorexic traits were kept under control.

Although it was terrifying to suddenly go from having total control to none at all, I knew deep down that I had already lost every ounce of control to the illness, and it was a relief not to be able to give into the anorexia's rules, despite this making the illness very angry.

The charge nurse picked up on me not having all of my margarine and also complained that I was walking around too much; they were watching me in the garden with my parents; it's like my every move is recorded!

I had to sit alone for breakfast with the supervising nurse, who told me off for putting too much butter on one piece of toast, and not enough on the other – arrgh! I feel like a naughty little child who has to be taught how to eat like a lady all over again, and at dinner when I went to cut my sandwich, the supervising nurse almost had a cow, leapt up in horror and said, appalled, 'No, No, No! This is how you eat your sandwich!' Good Lord, I almost killed the poor woman!

I felt I had done enough eating in front of an audience for one day: Will she or won't she? How will she perform today?

I often felt that I couldn't win with the nurses; trying to please them just wouldn't happen. I would either be eating too fast or too slow, be too anxious or too spaced out; I was outraged when they couldn't give me a decent enough excuse to explain why my eating wasn't satisfactory during one meal, when the nurse reported I was giving off an 'anorexic vibe'!

I'm trying to ask the nurses who supervise me during meals how they feel I coped; one of them said I gave her an 'anorexic vibe' – I can't see how I'm meant to work on that! One other nurse said I drink too much during meals as if I'm trying to wash away the taste! I think here you can never please the nurses; they will always be looking for some way that I can improve, whether it is eating too slow or too fast, eating too large or too small mouthfuls, drinking too much or not enough, being subdued at mealtimes or over-chatting . . . they'll find something to comment on.

She commented on my butter tub not being completely empty despite me making a conscious effort to SCRAPE SCRAPE; I feel like an idiot who can't get the simplest thing right. I'm trying so hard in the mornings to SCRAPE all the butter, SCRAPE all the jam from the pot on to the toast, but there's still always PLENTY more they can see for me to put on it. The nurses acted very oblivious to the fact that I was promised to go off supervision today, and kept me on it, apparently doing what's 'best for me'.

I was so frustrated by this inability to satisfy them, but over time I came to learn that with the many different cases of anorexia they witness, and with so many twisted tricks used to get out of just one bite, they were right to be constantly suspicious.

I gave up trying to please them, as I knew I was only there for myself, and the real girl in me knew if I was struggling or not.

Doing it for me

One of the girls refused her snack, although one of the others kept pushing her to eat it, asking 'so when are you going to have it then?' It is frustrating to have to eat when other people refuse, but at the end of the day, their refusal to get better won't get them out of here!

One of the girls followed me to my room, sat down and asked seriously if she'd offended me . . . by not scraping her bowl of walnut tart thoroughly enough! I realized I don't care what other people do; at the end of the day I want to get better, no matter how much or how little people around me want to.

However, the nurses were there to protect us from our destructive illnesses, and were always available to talk through any problems we had, or simply to be a shoulder to cry on. They helped me to get out my feelings, and small comments on my improvements throughout recovery kept me uplifted through difficult times.

I had a session with one of the nurses where we discussed change. I admitted how I was finding it difficult (rather than NOT) finishing my Flora in the morning, and told her my morning toast routine of having one slice loaded with butter, and another loaded with jam, but we couldn't see any anorexic logic behind it. I may do it normally tomorrow (even amounts of butter and jam on each slice) to see how it makes me feel. God, you really do tear apart every action to see if it may potentially be tainted with anorexia!

Being watched

As my illness developed, I had become so ashamed of eating in front of people, as if I was showing them how weak I was, and breaking their expectations that I would not eat. Of course, when my parents were actually lucky enough to witness the rare occasion that I was eating, they would like to sit with me and would watch me out of relief. I took this negatively, and of course the more I concealed my eating, the more conscious everyone else became of what I ate.

It even got to a point when I was ashamed to go into the kitchen in case people thought I was eating, and so I would creep around making no noise, opening the fridge as quietly as I could, pretending I didn't exist.

When I was trying to prepare something I would want to be left alone, and would get extremely stressed and irritated if anyone tried to interfere.

At The Priory, they worked on addressing this.

On Friday, we are going out to the local shopping centre to tackle a fear; mine is to eat in front of other people who aren't eating. It sounds weird, but I'm so ashamed of eating in front of other people – what if they look at me in disgust and interpret me as a greedy slob?

I felt really scruffy as I ate my toastie at lunch, that people were watching me and thinking what a pig I was.

I had afternoon snack on the ward, but I found Caroline really wound me up as she kept staring and asking questions about my food – I was like, 'Have you not SEEN food before?' and then she said, 'So is that what you eat when you reach your maintenance weight?'

Cheeky cow, what the hell will she think of me when I do actually reach it?!

I think I was too sensitive about it and shouldn't take it to heart, but in my ears it's like someone siding with my anorexia, thinking I don't need to gain, when in reality I have quite a bit more to go!

I had dried fruit in vanilla custard, was nice without the audience.

I was proud to eat my snack of Fortijuce and chocolate bar (a truffle chocolate lolly which was so rich and delicious!) Felt ashamed when Mum was like 'I know she's had her snack; I smelt it!' – cringe.

Tea was chips and Quorn sausage followed by peaches and custard, which didn't fill me so I had my snack early, but felt so paranoid with Jo watching me with her eagle eyes – grrr. At least I challenged my shame of eating in front of others.

I found it difficult to make a sandwich out of the Waldorf salad as it kept falling out and getting messy. I felt like a scruff and felt paranoid that people were thinking 'what a minger!'.

I was able to work on this, accepting that every human being needs food for fuel, and eating is not a sign of lack of control, or a reason to be ashamed.

I had a snack in front of my parents and their friends! When I saw Mum watching me, I could see how happy and relieved she was, and the paranoia of feeling like I was being judged as a pig was not there.

Patients

In The Priory, my recovery was not only assisted by the staff, but also by the other patients. I finally met people who had the same feelings as me; the strange obsession and issues around food, and who listened without judgment when I told them the thoughts in my head. We shared stories of the experiences we had had from our illness, and gave support.

No one can understand an eating disorder unless they have lived the nightmare themselves, and to know that when I found something hard, the others really did find it just as hard, meant I had less of an excuse to back out of it.

It was such fantastic support to be with people who understood my pain, my loneliness, my sense of having lost everything I ever was – for people to nod in agreement when I shared the twisted thoughts in my mind, rather than glance at each other with raised eyebrows over how messed up I actually was.

The girls often congratulated me on the small steps I'd made in recovery, encouraging me to give myself a pat on the back over the small, yet essential improvements I had made.

I feel a bond with one of the other patients in particular, it feels great to be able to talk to her and share feelings and thoughts. It's nice to know that I'm not totally alone, experiencing this hell all by myself. I felt so isolated outside of here; it's nice to feel less of a freak!

Some of the girls were commenting on how wise I was and that I talk a lot of sense as if I'm really going to get better and am changing, which feels great to hear, especially when I'm not one hundred per cent sure of it myself!

I spent the afternoon with some of the other girls, relaxing and chatting in the pleasant sunshine, and they assured me that I was 'doing fantastically well' which made me feel great; they see me from an understanding level because they've all been where I've been, and we're all insiders of this illness, rather than onlookers. It's easier to recognize traits when you've done the same things yourself.

One of the girls came into my room and looked at photos of mine from the good old days without anorexia, saying I was pretty and never looked fat; obviously that made me feel a bit more secure about gaining weight back to how I was.

I feel privileged to encourage other patients and be there for them, without being influenced by their anorexia.

I chatted to Dad on the phone, crying when I told him about the newbie's struggles, feeling sad that such a nice person is being destroyed by her illness, I found it tough to see her harm herself in the dining room.

Listening to some of the other girls and what they've been through made me realize how lucky I've been in not having gone through any huge trauma, and that suffering only makes you stronger.

I could see one of the new girls and how uncomfortable she was eating; shovelling it in like it was a plate of shit and thumping herself after each mouthful to punish herself. She came up from the dining hall a lot later after being sick.

Holly was such a sweetie, reminding me that going back

now would mean having to climb the ladder all over again. This is just a little, hard, blip, but it will be OK.

As I progressed in my recovery, I became increasingly aware of the situations in which my illness grasped a stronger hold over me: the times when I let my guard down, thinking it was over, it would spring back in full force.

Triggers are not necessarily the same for every sufferer of an eating disorder, but many are similar, and allow sufferers to be able to connect with each other, and give each other support in these difficult situations.

Family and friends

One thing that really helped me through the toughest stages of my recovery was the support of my family.

I remember my family coming to visit, and my total shame at having to be taken around in the wheelchair, and then slowly up the stairs to the eating disorder unit in the cringe-worthy stair lift. I thought 'I'm not an old lady! How degrading', but I think the true horror of what state I had got myself into was what really made me ashamed. After such a long time of compromising on eating food by doing exercise to compensate, it felt horrible to be shifted around, hardly moving, whilst the amount of food just built up inside me, energy unable to be burnt off.

Lots of my family came and visited today; a wonderful liberation from the dank atmosphere of the ward. My sister-in-law brought me chocolates as a present; but we are not allowed any food to be brought in for us so I had to say thanks, but no thanks! All the family came into my room on the unit and laughed and jumped on my new bed: it is an air mattress which sounds like it's about to take off and if you sit on one side, it sinks and rises on the other side. It's rather depressing that I need it to prevent getting bed sores, but I found it hilarious to see how much fun they were having on it! Everyone looks so happy and healthy: it's like I'm seeing my nephew Tom after not having seen him for so many months throughout my illness – he's so full of life that it's refreshing to see him.

This is not just a fight against anorexia, but a way of becoming stronger and discovering my true self. As strange as it sounds, I feel the least anorexic that I have in a long time. What doesn't kill us makes us stronger.

Mum helped me to be more patient about the weight gain; allow the stomach to fill out like a larder, then soon the fat will disperse elsewhere, and I will even out nicely.

It sounds kind of strange, but it helped me to be patient, to know that I wouldn't always have a tubby belly yet still scraggly arms and legs.

As the anorexia developed, I became like a little child again with my mother; very clingy and needy – at the same time, the relationships with other family members, such as my nephew and my brother-in-law were neglected, as I didn't have the energy to maintain them.

Hearing that my nephew always worried that I would die really hit home, and I decided then and there that I would get better to get to know my nephew once again, the boy that I'd grown up with like we were siblings.

I'm really aware of taking advantage of my parents; this is the age when I should be so much more independent, instead I rely on them more than ever. Had a refreshing fruit salad snack, but I know deep down it wasn't enough, and felt paranoid when Dad asked me what I ate.

On the weekend all my family are coming down to see me; my aunt, sister, brother-in-law, their baby, Mum, Dad, Kev, Tom, Toula . . . I can't help feeling like it'd be way too much for me. All these people! But we'll see. I'm just worried about how anti-social I am when I'm down.

Being used to the quiet, subdued environment of the hospital, it was difficult to be confronted by too many people; particularly when they all came to see me at once! I couldn't cope with so many visitors, and often got nervous of seeing people that knew me.

I met up with Helen for an hour or so; I can see in her eyes that she's pleased there is more me and less illness now. It was so lovely to see her, but I feel exhausted after even a little time with someone I haven't seen for a while, and kept it short.

Lots of the girls agreed that it's so difficult when you see too many outsiders in a short space of time, and congratulated me on managing to cope as well as I did. I felt I was really anti-social and distant with my brother-in-law, and sad that we have lost the strong bond that we used to have.

It was easier to relax with Mum today as it felt less frantic, and I was relieved that there were less people as it was way too much for me yesterday. I feel the relationship between me and my brother-in-law has

died; I don't have anything to say, his priority being work
and mine is myself.

However, as my recovery progressed, and I started to
visit home, I noticed a change: I was willing to make an
effort with others, and also a lot more comfortable in
my own skin.

Toula came round, seeming tired and overworked, and for
some reason I felt the perfectionist mask coming on felt
especially anxious when I found out we had guests
staying for tea. But I made a yummy salad (dressed with
mango, stilton, grapes and cashews) and Mum cooked
chicken, made tomato salad and peas and sweetcorn, so
was nice to join in. She made a cake for dessert which I
wasn't too fussed about, so I ate some and left a bit. We
chatted for a bit, then watched TV, having a laugh over
'You've Been Framed' and deluded people on 'The X
Factor'. Eva came round and me, her, Tom and Mum
watched 'The Devil Wears Prada'. I felt really close to
them all, able to relax and so happy to be there.

I was very lucky that even in the worst stages of my
illness, many of my friends and family still stuck by me.
I think that you don't have to be anorexic to suffer as a
result of it, and I am amazed that people could stick by

the person that they knew and loved as they deteriorated and changed into someone – something – completely different. I didn't know myself, yet they helped me pull through by having faith in me.

In the worst year of the anorexia, I did not make any new friends (and lost many), but through recovery I began to regain social interests and confidence amongst people; these changes became apparent in hospital.

I received a lot of mail from friends and family wishing me strength, and reminding me of my capabilities without the illness. As motivation, I stuck these cards around my room, as they were constant reminders of those who cared about me, and reasons for me to persevere with my recovery through the hard times.

This week, I think one of my friends is coming to see me, which I'm unexplainably nervous about.

A new patient who is not in the eating disorder unit but has problems with her eating came to sit on my table at dinner today; she seemed very agitated like she couldn't keep still, but she's so lovely and invited me to come and hang out with her when I have the freedom to. She says her brother saw me and thought I was gorgeous! How anyone could think that I'll never know, but I felt pleased all the same.

This evening my friend came to visit and although I was anxious about seeing her, it was actually really lovely. It wasn't at all awkward and she only had compliments about how I'm looking better – I appreciate her acknowledgement of my progress.

Chapter Four

Mealtimes

There was such a horrible vibe during mealtimes at hospital as no one wanted to be there, and everyone found the situation just as terrifying as the next person. Dinners were often awkward, uncomfortable occasions, with a nurse trying to juggle making tedious conversation as a means of distraction, watching to make sure everyone was eating with the correct etiquette, and pacing their own meal to the slowness of the reluctant eaters.

The atmosphere at the dining table was horrific: everyone sitting there looking miserable and trying to be as slow as possible, making mundane conversation. It's horrible sitting there when I know my family are having a wonderfully relaxed conversation just in the room next door.

Not only was there an awkward vibe, but the eating times were very strict, and a slight delay coming into the dining room would not be acceptable. This rigidity enabled me to feed myself when it was time to eat, not just on the rare occasion that I felt hungry. (Now, the anxiety produced if a meal is slightly earlier or later than I had 'planned' has reduced considerably, as I am aware that in reality, it isn't realistic to expect food to be prepared exactly at the right time each day. I no longer allow strict food regimes to run my life and emotions, although it is important to remember to eat and not busy yourself to avoid eating times.)

Today, my family arrived at 12.50 instead of 12.30 which is normal lunchtime, and I'm so trained to eating dead on time that I felt really anxious, and had to start eating before they came.

Got stuck in DREADFUL standstill traffic when we were meant to be back for tea. I could feel myself getting stressed, and my parents getting anxious that we wouldn't be back in time for tea, but I stopped myself from looking at the clock, relaxed my body and accepted the fact that we would be late, but that was the way it was today. It's unrealistic to expect food to be spot on time every day, because in the real world, mealtimes aren't the be-all and end-all of the daily routine! We ended up fifteen minutes late, but all was well, and I enjoyed my turkey stir fry.

I felt quite self-conscious in front of men in the restaurant, worried about the set menu of three courses, so I limited myself on each course. It took forty minutes for our starters to arrive; I was going mad! We finished about 10.30 – I did get very anxious about the time and wished they'd hurry up, but the food was nice and it was lovely to catch up with my friend.

Menu

At The Priory, the menu was carefully planned and decided by the hospital dietician. The menu was organized in such a way that we had some choice, but the main structure of the meals was fixed, and there was no room for the anorexia to swoop in and restrict our intake – although I recognized that many indecisive moments on my part were due to the illness panicking over which option I should choose, reminding me that to not choose anything at all would be the easy way out, and far more guilt free.

Breakfast was a bowl of cereal and two pieces of toast with butter and jam; which cereal and jam flavour being your choices.

Lunch was titled a 'snack meal'; a sandwich accompanied by a fruit juice or a packet of crisps, followed by a heavy, cake-like pudding drenched in custard for dessert.

Dinner was a larger main meal including all food groups, such as a pork dinner with gravy, followed by a lighter pudding such as bananas in custard.

Every lunch and dinner had two options of meals which we selected each morning; one option including meat, and the other a vegetarian option, yet still providing the same nutritional benefits.

A good thing about the dietician is how she is so blunt; there's no room for the anorexia with this woman, and once you increase your portion size, then that's that. Once you choose a meal, then that's what you're having.

I feel very intimidated by the dietician, probably because I know she has control over the thing that I fear most: she can increase my diet as she pleases. She must have one of the hardest jobs – I can't imagine being a dietician in an eating disorder unit is particularly easy!

Was weigh day this morning, but I'm not allowed to know my weight. If it's going up, my diet stays the same, but if it goes down – uh-oh – diet increase! I chatted to the dietician who structured an increase in my diet, and I feel more connected to her now, like we've established what's what.

There was an hilarious uproar in the canteen today; those who had chosen something other than the chocolate mousse on the Eating Disorder menu had the other 'large dessert', whereas I, who would have been happy with mousse, ended up having a choc ice which is a 'small dessert', and I was happy with that. But ohh noo! Heads were turning, nurses were parading around very angry that the regularity of the normal meal plan was disrupted.

With patients that entered the eating disorder unit severely starved, the diet was started at just a quarter of the regular portions, to allow the person's stomach and mind to be able to adjust to this increased quantity of food.

However, I was shocked to see the small portion sizes, and was consumed by this strong hunger, to such an extent that I actually moaned to the nurses about being too hungry, and wanting my diet increased! It didn't make sense to me to be hungry in an eating disorder unit, as this was the place in which I wanted to start my physical recovery as soon as possible. Perhaps the small, frequent meals awoke my appetite.

Because I have hardly been eating, they started me off with a portion size a quarter the size of everyone else's – couldn't believe how small it was! At 8 in the evening we had a snack, and I'm not allowed anything off the snack menu like chocolate or biscuits, but I had to have a high calorie supplement drink. Lunch was a quarter cheese and pickle sandwich and a spoonful of apple crumble and custard, dinner quarter of a Quorn sausage, a sprig of broccoli and a few chips. I wasn't allowed condiments or even extra veg! I couldn't understand, and afterwards I bawled into Mum's shoulder, as I scrunched up in my bed, freezing cold.

Still had a quarter portion for breakfast which I wolfed down as it was so small, but got a half portion of pizza and salad for lunch. I got a bit told off by one of the other patients for talking about food and wanting to see the menu – in an eating disorder unit, the 'f' word is 'food'! Ridik. I'm so freezing cold and have a chill in my bones which I don't think will ever leave me, and the backs of my knees are so sore from muscle wastage, but I'm not going to admit that. I'm so pissed off; I went to look for the dietician to ask if I could have an increased meal portion as I was so hungry. I guess now that my metabolism is kicking in and my food amount is still very small, I'm bound to feel hungry. However she wasn't in, and no one else is allowed to change your diet plan – so poor old hungry me had to stick through it! It's almost laughable – hungry in an eating disorder unit?!

I kicked up a big fuss about how hungry I was, because I woke up so hungry. All the other girls thought I was being difficult but I didn't care; I managed to get a supplement drink which kept the angry stomach rumblings at bay.

I felt compelled to write down my daily intake of food, partly due to an anorexic obsession, but I think I was genuinely amazed at the amount I could eat without ballooning catastrophically.

I'm all excited to try the foods that 'Ali' loves but couldn't eat with the anorexia, like Nutella which I miss sooo much! Today's munch record:
Bowl of Alpen, two slices toast with Flora and blackcurrant jam
Blueberry muffin, supplement drink
Prawn, seafood and lettuce sandwich. Walnut tart and custard
Dairy Milk bar, supplement drink (missed my apple though)
Pork chop, mashed potato, cabbage, apple sauce and gravy (surprisingly nice and not too big although it sounds like a lot!)

*Fruit fool (probably one of my favourite desserts but I had
to gulp it down as my aunt was waiting to take me out!)
Fruit salad and cream*

We were given the opportunity to have three 'dislikes':
commonly selected were things like cream. Often,
patients chose their fear foods as dislikes to avoid eating
them, and I often found a lot of turbulence with my
dietician who believed I was simply avoiding food,
rather than disliking it, and this frustrated me. After
food being my main source of control in life, I felt I was
being walked over, people ignoring the person inside
the anorexic body, and assuming all my opinions were
silly little anorexic behaviours.

*I put stewed fruit as my dislike but they bunged a fruit
crumble in front of me, ignoring my protests. I felt so
upset and anxious that I burst out crying, but trying
desperately to keep a lid on it. Some of the girls were
sympathetic and supportive, telling me they were with me
'on every bite of that crumble' – so sweet, and great to
feel understood.*

*Lunch dessert today was choc ice – my dislike – so I put
down fruit salad and sorbet, the alternative, and when
I received choc ice, I looked confused and asked the*

nurse who acted all Innocent. I know this morning on the menu she didn't bother to tell the kitchen that it was my dislike. But I ate it anyway to avoid kicking up a fuss, and annoyed with myself for allowing people to walk all over me.

We arrived back in time for lunch, and once again they attempted to give me stewed fruit dessert (apple crumble) because they didn't have the information from the dietician that my dislikes had changed. But I REFUSED to eat it, and the waitress soon scurried out with a bowl of fruit salad when I got up to tell one of the therapists.

Ruth [dietician] came for a chat, annoyed at me because the waitresses had been saying I only order fruit salad and yoghurt for dessert: I only did yesterday instead of fruit crumble. She thinks I'm avoiding these puddings and says it shouldn't have taken me so long to choose it as a dislike – I said I didn't realize there was a time limit to choose our dislikes! Even though she wasn't happy with me having crumble as a dislike, out of sheer stubbornness I stuck to it. Now my dislikes are ice cream, sorbet and crumble: lovely. I totally stuck up for myself, not allowing her to put me down – she had told me it was OK to have 'frozen dessert' and 'stewed fruit' as

66

dislikes and now I'm getting told off for it! Which I won't stand for.

After a session with my dietician, I feel frustrated and angry that I'm trying so hard, eating everything that's asked of me without refusing or throwing a strop, and she accused me of struggling and said that nurses that supervise me during meals are saying I'm finding it difficult with desserts! I have absolutely no control over eating situations, and this frustrates me.

At lunch today the waitress brought me my dislike, Viennetta, so I put my foot down, feeling so angry towards the nurse who had told the kitchen that I would be having that, even though she KNOWS it's a dislike! I want to sort this out with the dietician but talking to her means something bad has happened; we have an argument, I've lost weight, she ups my diet etc.

Sometimes it's difficult to distinguish why you select certain foods to eat; whether you genuinely prefer a lower calorie meal, or whether your illness is forcing you into having the smaller option. Being brought up with a healthy diet, I am such a lover of fruit, and would always opt for a fruit salad over a chocolate bar. I found it difficult to choose what I wanted, and often chose the opposite just in case it was the illness that had wanted it.

For dinner, I tried the beef and mushroom cobbler which to my surprise I really enjoyed – and I tell myself I don't even like beef! This time, the nurse told me I ate well and at a good pace.

Home-made rice pudding dessert was surprisingly nice: for so long the illness has told me that I 'don't like' certain foods like beef, pasta or rice, but now that I have to eat them I do actually enjoy them, and realize they're just fear foods.

Depending on our weights, we were given supplement drinks to help us restore to our maintenance weights, and I got up to having three a day, with two snacks from the snack menu. I strongly disagreed with the choices of snacks, all of which I thought were nutritionally empty and some form of junk food. I felt my opinion on it was not taken seriously – it was easy to read my dislike of these snacks as simply a way of my anorexia allowing me to escape junk food, but in reality, I had been brought up on healthy, nutritious meals, and considered chocolate and sweets an occasional treat. Definitely not something to indulge in three times a day!

At snack today when I bit into my fruitcake, I had the most horrendous tooth pain. I'm really paranoid that the amount of junk – cakes, jam, sugary cereals and chocolate – are going to rot my teeth.

Numbers

For so long my diet was dictated to me depending on the numbers on the back of packets, that it took a lot of effort and challenging of my anorexic behaviour to not look at the nutritional content of food.

We bought some munchies from Marks and I accidentally drank a 275kcal fizzy drink, forgetting to check if it was a diet drink! I was horrified!

I'm so tempted to work out how many calories are in certain foods here, but that is the anorexia trying to scare me about how much more I'm eating compared to before I was hospitalized. I challenged myself with this thought by remembering how awful life became after limiting calories obsessively; the numbers on the back of a packet would determine whether I bought it or not. Look how much I've developed both mentally and physically, just over three weeks of a high cal, non-controlled diet! I never needed to limit my calorie intake in the first place, as it disadvantaged me in so many ways:

they're unimportant and meaningless as is weight, and only need to be considered when they're dangerously low or high.

A personal problem for me was my focus on fat, and wanting to cut down on it as much as I possibly could. During transition from being an inpatient to a day patient, I was still unable to control my food intake during main mealtimes, but as a day patient, I was allowed to select my own snack choices, and as a result found an old anorexic behaviour creeping back in; the compulsion to cut back on as much fat as possible. I would often decide which snack I was to have depending on its fat content, opting for things like dried fruit or sweets.

I developed a habit of collecting and listing nutritional information on the various snacks, and allowed myself to be influenced over whether they were the 'good' choices, or the naughtier choices. Eventually, I was able to admit what I was doing.

I have a snack confession to make; I didn't finish my supplement drink at afternoon snack, and 'forgot' a few Maltesers at the bottom of the packet; ever since I saw an advert for one packet being less than 180kcal, that means in two packets there are almost 400kcal and that's wayyy more than the necessary 300kcal which snack is supposed to be. I wish the numbers didn't decide what or how much I ate. It was a horrible realization of the anorexia creeping in; cutting corners to see if I could get away with it. It's so hard to push out that little voice, especially when you don't know whether it's you that would rather the lower kcal option, or the illness. For example, I thought I wanted Bran Flakes, and was influenced to choose this by the little voice that piped up 'and they're only 150kcal compared to 180kcal in Fruit and Fibre!'. To prove my recovery doesn't mean I have to eat the most calorific item on the menu all the time, it means having what I want.

I felt like I'd made the wrong decision for dinner, but soon forgot it and put it to the back of my mind. I'm tempted to update and read my anorexic page listing the fat and calorie content of each snack, but I know I'll be very annoyed with myself if I do this.

I sneakily saw the saturated fat contents in my chocolate muffin but I didn't write it in my anorexic page of snack calculations. Today I won't write my food intake as I know it's the anorexia obsessing.

I browsed potential snacks, like a Malteser drink, animal

biscuits and custard pots. Very conscious of the fat content although I know I DON'T have to look!

I try to reduce the amount of fat I have in snacks, in a huge dilemma between Galaxy (15g) and Milky Way/Mars Delight (10g); the choice is overwhelming! At the end of the day, I ended up having 17g fat in snacks; very low for here, before I was having more like 80g.

I told the nurse about my anorexic nutritional value page, and how I haven't looked at it all week, and when she asked me where it was I told her I'd thrown it, which was a teeeensy lie but it's what I have to do – now! So I did it, and felt strangely satisfied and strong, even a sense of relief!

Even a year on after leaving hospital, I often glance at the nutritional value as a decider for tiny choices, such as which new yoghurt to try, or which cereal to have this week. However, I am now aware of the negative associations I have with fat and calories, and ban myself from looking at these details, opting to try foods which have other nutritional benefits, such as high fibre cereal, or soya products – rich in calcium.

After learning more about the beneficial aspects of nutrition, I was able to use the high amount of particular nutrients as a way of exploring new foods, until I no longer needed to read the back of a packet. I was aware that nothing awful would happen by not reading the calorie or fat content, so why not opt for something I truly want? I feel very proud to have done a whole supermarket sweep without once glancing at the back of a packet!

Some very important advice that I strongly recommend to any recoverer is to ignore numbers, whether it is the numbers on the scale, on the back of a packet or on an exercise apparatus; even the hands on a clock! Although a very hard step to take, and it may feel that you're losing control, I found it much less of a burden to not know my weight, and less panicked when I was told it was increasing.

It's great to be able to enjoy something without feeling a subtle niggle of guilt, if I don't know the calorie content. The key is to remembering that a 'normal' diet involves a wide variety of foods to have the best nutritional advantage, and one day, having a bit more or less does not necessarily make a huge difference to your weight.

Chapter Five

A Healthy Body and Mind

You only truly appreciate health when it is too late. I have damaged my circulation, and as an effect have Reynaud's syndrome, which, much to my embarrassment, turns my hands and feet into a startling array of colours. Although I feel grateful that I haven't suffered more severely in the long term – as many sufferers of eating disorders do – it is a constant reminder of the punishment I have put my body through.

Sharp pangs of pain in my kidneys, the threat of infertility, the inability to look at boys in the same way as my friends: however petty or extreme, these are all reality checks that made me realize I have two options – to allow myself to be bullied into a life of misery, ill health and pain by something inside my own head; or, pushing on through a constant battle with myself (often feeling like shit and thinking that to go back would be easier) but possibly, somewhere in the future, seeing a tiny speck of a beautiful light at the end of the tunnel. Pushing on through was far from easy, but was the best decision I have ever made. I have seen the brighter days, and that life can continue after anorexia.

Size and identity – mind not body

One of the most difficult things about being a sufferer of an eating disorder is that although you're ill, people can still see you and not the strange, destructive force inside of you.

'Why is she doing this to herself?' people would wonder, as they gawped at the skeletal figure that marched down the street past them.

Many people assume that a skinny body means that you're anorexic, but what people often forget is that anorexia is a *mental* illness, and it's the effect of the maladaptive thoughts that make the body so shockingly thin. It is often only a cause for concern when the mental breakdown begins to become visible, and can no longer be ignored.

I felt so ashamed of my frail, scraggly body, yet at the same time, terrified to gain weight and lose my anorexic identity. After all, the illness was all I had been for so long, and all people had expected from me, so apart from the illness, who was I?

One of the girls described recovery as slowly chipping away at the person you want to become until eventually, a new figure and identity appear, but only through consistency, patience and determination can the figure develop. She also said that recovery is like sitting on a ridge with steep drops on each side; you know how awful it would be to fall back to where you were – back to the illness – but at the same time you're terrified to enter the unknown land of recovery as it involves so many challenges and risks.

I sought reassurance in feeling my skeletal body; reassurance to know that I still 'felt anorexic', therefore I hadn't strayed too far from my anorexia's control and rules.

One of the girls told me that if she saw me as a stranger on the street, she'd still think I had an eating disorder, and I was strangely comforted and relieved by this twisted mind of mine!

By chatting to one of the outpatients, she made me realize that my always touching my bones, and being reassured by my emaciation that I am still skinny even when I feel full, is only the anorexia trying to make me feel the need to look so malnourished. I need to tell myself that this sick body is the result of an illness, not something that should give me reassurance or relief.

My stomach often feels full and bloated, but touching it and obsessing about how many extra millimetres it has grown won't make me a healthier person; I look forward to a healthy, nourished, feminine body that I love, look after and feel comfortable in.

I do get nervous about feeling really full although I don't like my figure now; I think I'm really unattractive and skinny – but when I start to feel like I'm putting on weight I know I'm going to panic. It's the fat on my stomach that scares me the most. In particular, I hate feeling that my hip bones aren't protruding. I'm confused because although I want my hipbones to show, I want extra padding when I sit down, I want curves and boobs etc. I'm scared to lose the motivation I have so strongly now to get better, and when this goes, how am I going to cope without the protection of looking thin?

People often perceive the media as having a huge effect on anorexia, on the striving to be thin and attractive like the models. Personally, I could see the severity of the thinness of the models, and never aspired to imitate that, but I did aspire to be accepted, and perhaps irrationally believed that being thinner would make me 'fit in' more.

Anorexia may be considered acceptable on the catwalk, but this only considers the bodies on parade and nothing of the mental and emotional torment that goes on backstage, in the minds of the sufferers when they are stripped of expensive clothes and lavish make-up.

I had a chat to a day-patient who I have developed quite a close friendship with. She's really struggling, not managing her snacks or pudding at lunch, because she feels she's happy at the weight she is. The thing is though, you have to learn that it's not the weight that's making you happy, because the anorexia will never be happy at the weight you are: it's always about being what you're not – a couple of pounds lighter, completely perfect – but is impossible.

I visualise the illness as a growth or deformity that lives in the last vertebra of my spine. It's rotting and disgusting, like a cancer that has grown over time and has stopped me doing all the things that I love to do. Physically, it is only small in size, but it has taken over my world and engulfed me. I can smell this rotting, foul smell that haunts me wherever I go no matter how hard I try to conceal it. Others can sense it too, but out of embarrassment and to avoid an awkward situation they say nothing, instead they just find being with me too difficult and eventually stop spending time with me.

It's latched on so strongly like a leech that If I was to remove it, I couldn't distinguish between what is me and what is it. The pain is horrendous; every time I sit or lie down I am reminded of its physical presence. I am a coward because I know the process of removing it will be difficult, but I know its strength – I know if I allow it to grow it will eventually kill me, but it tempts me because it promises to protect me, and it's the safer option to follow to avoid feelings of self disgust and guilt.

I can't identify its words but its instructions are clear, as are the warnings of what will happen if I were to rebel. To be honest, I'm not entirely sure what will happen, but I know it will hurt and won't be worth it. If I need reassurance from it, I can feel it physically in my body and am flooded with a sense of relief by touching the bones. I'm terrified of the thought of not having the physical presence which makes people aware there is a problem, because I know it will still be there even if it's not apparent to others.

I'm starting to become aware that this fight will be so hard mentally; putting on weight is the easiest part because

I'm simply recovering from a symptom of the illness, and not the illness itself. I won't be recovered from the illness until I've been a year at my maintenance body weight, and that feels almost impossibly far away. My skinny appearance makes me feel protected and hidden, but at the same time I want to look better. I find it hard to compare myself to other people's sizes; others are allowed to be normal sized but I feel I have to look thin to look delicate, neat and acceptable.

Weight loss is simply an outcome of the illness that is going on in the mysterious depths of the sufferer's mind, and the severity of the anorexia should by no means be measured by the sufferer's size, as often the anorexia is far worse when the physical body appears well.

With such a high focus on diets, losing weight and shaping up, in society today, it is difficult not to get brainwashed, and very tempting to excuse yourself from a meal just because a friend skipped lunch, or someone else isn't eating. I would feel embarrassed at the amount I had to eat to gain a healthy weight, and when I wasn't accompanied during meals, the temptation to not eat was always there.

When people say things such as how little they've eaten that day, or what diet they're on, it is difficult to hear, but in reality, there is such a strong, distorted thinking on dieting and health that these types of discussions are unavoidable in the real world.

The important thing is to be aware of the meaning of a skipped meal for a person with an eating disorder. This isn't just a few corners of nutrition cut and made up for later, this is holding on to anorexia for dear life, allowing it to sooth your momentary anxiety, letting it take control over the sufferer, and once it gets comfortable, it doesn't like to budge easily. It's too easy for problems to escalate and for you to start slipping, and the illness will be only too happy to take back control. Indulging in anorexic behaviour is a constant temptation, but it's something that the illness will feed off, and like putting sticks on a fire, you're only encouraging it to grow. Don't give it the opportunity to have that grip over you again, and ignore that competitive rush; certainly don't feel that you need to be dieting too.

Despite wanting to be thin, and actually associating the feeling of thinness with feeling satisfied and content, I didn't want any of the associated issues. Thinness is no compensation for the feelings of guilt and shame that swarmed over me with every bite that passed my lips.

I can remember how awful I felt in my anorexic body

trapped by my anorexic mind, and when I find myself giving into anorexic temptations, I use this as motivation to get out of the situation, as I never want to go back to rock bottom. If you can't remember it yourself, others will tell you how bad it was. I am consciously aware of how much better I feel within myself and in my physical appearance.

Even now, in the later stages of recovery, I worry that when recovery is over, when my weight is restored and the illness is no longer such a threat, what will I think about? What identity will I have then? I often see recovery as a project, and wonder what would be the replacement project. I've realized that all the normal things, from gossiping with my friends, to really contemplating what career path I want to take in life, would be the new project; life in itself would be my new project, and not the illness.

During this illness, people can never win. The sufferer can never lose enough weight. Nobody can ever understand. Even those who love you the most can't get a simple compliment right. For example, so many patients would be terrified and panicked by being told they were 'looking better' because what does better mean? To the anorexic, it means you are steering too far from the illness. You are starting to look normal, so people won't be careful around you. They won't treat you delicately, and won't give you second chances. Even in the later stages of recovery when I no longer went to The Priory, a simple comment such as my mum saying I'd eaten well would throw me into a frenzy of questions:

Have I eaten too much?

Do people think I'm a pig?

Are they disgusted by how far I'm straying from my anorexia, my control?

My aunt came to see me today and tried to pay me a compliment by saying my face seemed fuller – immediately I interpreted this as a negative point – am I already so fat after so little time as an inpatient?! I soon realized this was the anorexia making me think that this was a criticism, and it stopped me from accepting a compliment, it stopped me from regaining any self-worth or confidence. I challenged this thought of 'Oh God, I must look so fat!' by thinking of all the times I've felt ashamed of my scraggly, skinny body of bones, and looked forward to rebuilding a more attractive, healthy, HUMAN face!

I don't know where I stand with this illness any more, it's as if I'm blinded by my motivation to get better to the fact that I'm still ill, and when I realize that I'm still very much anorexic and have such a long way to go before full recovery, I get disappointed and angry at myself, feeling that there's no point in pushing on as it will only get harder as the weight increases. It's as if I have to be ignorant of the extent of my illness to remain motivated. I can't seem to find a happy medium between acceptance and motivation.

My sister-in-law said I was looking healthier, and this is a positive thing; sometimes you get so sucked into being a fragile, ill person that feels hidden from the cruel world by anorexia, that it's scary to recover, and it's frightening that people can see your improvement.

Feeling fat and full

The feeling of fat is more of a panic, deep inside, which bubbles up and takes full control of your mind, so that it is all you can think about. You feel sheer terror, repulsed by the content that sits heavily in your stomach, terrified at what it might do to you, but above all, terrified about the lack of control that you have experienced by simply eating. The feeling of fullness brought this anxiety up for me; I would feel restless and often need a distraction to keep my mind from focusing on my uncomfortable feeling.

When you don't feel like eating, look a bit deeper and see what you're really feeling: anger, hurt, upset? The feeling of fat means the anorexia is hiding your true feelings from you, so that it can become that little bit stronger inside. Most of the things that you enjoy, the illness will not enjoy, so it is about making that choice; are you going to please your illness, or yourself?

Earlier, I was talking to Mum about what I thought my ideal weight would be for my height and got teary and panicky because I know how much I hate myself at that weight. I need to feel like I'm digesting and the food isn't just sitting in a disgusting lump in my stomach, dissolving through my body into fat. I'm awful for comparing myself with others, and when I see other people's fat I feel terrified; I know that if that were me I'd feel miserable and hate myself; with anorexia I will never be exposed to these horrible feelings because with it, I won't get fat. I feel safe with anorexia. I recognize that when my leg shakes, when I take a few extra steps more than I should and I need to, or when I'm particularly restless, this is the anorexia trying to burn up any excess energy that might get me fat. I need to fight these habits and soon it will gradually become easier to get the illness out of my system. Anorexia is NOT my friend; it's destroying my life and tearing my mind apart. But feeling full is the signal to my anorexia that something's not right, and it needs to start putting its point across.

I feel like I'm mindlessly eating – when will I realize I'm gaining weight and panic? Is it wrong to expect myself to panic? Last night I felt ill and the fullest I've ever felt here, but I went to have my supplement drink and although I felt physically disgusting, I felt proud of myself for fighting the anorexia which was tempting me to cut back.

I feel each bite I take is taking me that extra little bit closer to gaining weight and reaching recovery, and I'm confident that recovery does not mean getting fat. It means getting healthy and back to a normal life!

The deluded sense that the illness gives you makes you feel in control from refusing temptation – and being able to resist something I really wanted was like a show of willpower. People often remarked on my willpower and determination, yet as the illness developed, it became clear to everyone including myself, that the anorexia had used these personality traits to its advantage, and stolen any true control I might have had. Having learnt more about my illness, I've realized that true control is being able to eat even when the illness instructs me not to.

I talked to Mum who told me that by telling myself 'I CAN'T' only makes the struggle harder, if I just get on with it and tell myself 'I CAN' then I will. It's using the willpower that got me ill, but in a positive way. By listening to this advice, the nerves and irritation I was expecting to feel after eating the snack were replaced with surprise over how easy it was.

I know that lying to myself will only make the illness stronger, but I can't help knowing it will be hard. Fight the illness! Fight for you and for recovery, and you WILL destroy your demon bully.

I can still recall the discomfort of my belly, unadjusted to the amount of food that was in it, and the anxiety that I would normally distract myself from by exercise was so much stronger.

I felt extremely fretful to have to eat two packets of Maltesers and a supplement drink after a Sunday lunch – nobody eats like that, it feels so piggish.

Put on my skinny jeans this morning, which are most definitely skinny fit now! I'm starting to feel big around my stomach and love handle area; hopefully it's just the jeans!

87

Feeling my weight gain quite a lot, feel like my shirt is about to burst open and I feel about 8st, whereas when I calculated it I'm more like 7½st. I'm starting to want to slow down the weight gain, feeling uncomfortable in my ever-expanding body. Apparently I'm still in a state of starvation even when I'm re-feeding, which makes me prone to obsessing about food and to binge.

I think I'm starting to feel my weight gain, every now and then on my stomach I notice it's a lot more round, and foldy! I've felt really full all day too, which probably doesn't help.

Just come back from going out for a pizza and a browse on Park Street, still very full and about to have 600kcal of Fortijuce – argh! Really tempted to skip one so as to only have four snacks, but one of the therapists warned me that now I'm reaching the weight where I'll want to stop gaining, but I must hang on in there.

Lunch was spaghetti hoops on toast; I felt SO full after just a quarter of the toast and the thought of having to plough through that AND dessert was horrible, yet I got on with it. I went for a walk on my own to try and ease the fullness.

The illness made me feel horrible about myself; I hated what I looked like and was disgusted with both weight loss and weight gain. Asking myself honestly, being 5 stone or 9 stone, I was unhappy with myself, regardless of the number that the scale read. I had deeper, underlying issues which needed to be addressed before even contemplating the image that the mirror showed me.

By accepting how awful the illness is making you feel, and staying with it, the negativity and focus does gradually diminish. I avoid body checking, and prefer to not know my weight, as I know my illness would be dissatisfied with any number on the scale. It's important to remember that a varied, well-balanced diet will get me a healthy weight, body and mind set.

Exercise

We have all been there: it's a cold, dark morning outside and you lie tucked up in your cosy, warm bed, moaning at the familiar, relentless, unwelcome screech of the alarm clock. Every nerve of your being is willing you to bat the alarm clock off the bedside table and turn back on to your pillow, but that niggle inside reminding you that it's not a matter of choice that you have to get up – that is the only thing that gets you hauling yourself out of the sheets and getting on with the day. That niggle –

whether it be the thought of your boss's angry face as you stroll in late, or the panic of having so much to do that day, or anorexia – it is there, and although only small, has the power to drive you against your will.

This is how I can best explain my absolute compulsion to exercise.

Now, imagine that you're already late when you wake up; as you glance at the clock, you're suddenly aware of the awful situation. Overslept again! Panic shoots through you as you hurtle into the shower and fly through the front door. You have no time in your mind to consider the luxury of lying in.

In the same way, I would wake up every morning always terribly late for my illness; it would wake me with its screams that I was never good enough and gave me a horrific sense of urgency.

Exercise is the one thing that I still feel compelled to do, and can excuse myself with the justification that exercise is healthy. Yes, exercise is good for you, but it is very important to be honest with yourself as to whether you are doing it for pleasure, or for the angry voice that taunts you in the back of your mind.

At home, I was once walking around the nearby park of my house and I came to a pathway that would lead back down the hill, giving me exactly thirty minutes' walking time, or there was an extended path that gave

Me (age 6) at a family meal in 1995

My seventh birthday party -
me in red at the end of the table

1996 - riding, aged about 7

On a school trip to London, aged 14, before anorexia

Summer 2005, aged 16, over the first bout of anorexia and about to go to college

September 2006, aged 17, with friends Anna and Tara before a night out

6 2007, at the worst of my illness 9

6 February 2008, celebrating my nineteenth birthday 9

me forty-five minutes' walking time. I could feel the temptation to just carry straight on and take the longer walk: besides, no one would even know, and I would feel momentarily better. But from past experience, I realized how, if I took that step towards the longer path, there was no going back; from that day on, the shorter path would never be acceptable, and it was only a matter of time before I would have to extend the new forty-five minute route.

If there's something I've learnt about the illness, it is that there is no bargaining with it; it does not appreciate your opinion. So, despite my anorexia becoming increasingly annoyed, and punishing me with taunts of laziness, I continued along the shorter path, pleased afterwards that I had given 'Ali' the opportunity to make a choice this time.

At The Priory, exercise was monitored like everything else.

I had a stack of papers in the garden, and before tea I went to put them back in my room, but another patient challenged me, asking, 'Do you really need to keep going up and down those stairs?' That annoyed me, that she was interfering with business that was nothing to do with her, but I do recognize how I walk around compulsively, and leave things in my room that I know I'll need just so I can come back up the stairs again. Tomorrow I'm going to count the number of times I go up and down the stairs unnecessarily. I have to have a decent reason to do it – it will be so easy to let it get out of control if I remain oblivious to the problem, and I find it embarrassing that people are noticing this trait; I am embarrassed to be anorexic.

However, once this choice has been made, the illness will try, again and again, to make its opinion heard. Just because I chose the right path that time does not make my compulsion to exercise any easier. It is a constant battle that the sufferer needs to stay aware of, as often, at times in which we feel least ill, the illness has the greatest way into your mind, and can catch you off guard with its sneaky passage back into control.

I got up and did forty situps – meant to do twenty but they weren't done properly – and I know it's the anorexia but I feel if I just keep my stomach toned, rather than burn off kcals, I'll feel better about myself. Rules?

I was rewarded for my weight gain in hospital by being allowed an increasing number of walks. I loved to move after feeling so full and stuffed with food – it served as a good distraction and also made me feel less guilty knowing that I was burning some of the fuel that I was so uncomfortably full with.

I can't enjoy food any more because I don't deserve to be having it now I'm so much bigger. I cried non-stop, even through dinner. I was picking at my BLT baguette and the girls told me they'd never seen me struggle like that before, even the slowest eaters had finished! I really had to shovel it down, which is difficult when you are crying and can't breathe! I finished chocolate mousse (FAT PIG), before going for another walk.

I'm dealing with the amount of food OK, sometimes I even look forward to meals because it's something to do, and because of this anticipation I think I may be susceptible to bingeing. I think, 'How the hell can I have eaten four slices of bread, a bowl of cereal and a high calorie supplement drink – and it's not even lunchtime yet?!' But I recognize that I NEED this food to fight the physical destruction of anorexia, before being able to go on and conquer the mental damage.

I came to realize that my happiness did not depend on the size that I was; I could be having a really difficult day and feel huge, and weeks later when I knew I had put on weight but was feeling more positive in myself, I would be happy with who I was.

Refeeding

After depriving your body of food for so long, there are often lots of side effects and changes that occur when the re-feeding process begins.

When trying to gain weight before I came to The Priory, I experienced a horribly off-putting oedema, which is basically water retention, and made me bloat up like a water balloon. I felt revolting, and often, pressing a patch on my leg would leave a dent of a finger mark there for several seconds before the water inside leveled it out. I was even more disgusted with myself, and unsurprisingly, I soon gave up on the attempted weight gain.

In the controlled environment of hospital, I luckily did not experience that again, although many other patients did.

My body temperature rose from a painfully low 33 degrees to more reasonable levels and I was able to walk around in sleeveless tops; something I hadn't been able to do in years! I would wake up soaked in sweat as I became so hot in the nights. From some bizarre reasoning, I felt the need to keep my body temperature as low as possible, so that I could burn calories in my body's attempt to keep warm, so nurses would often force me to bring jumpers if I were to leave my room.

In some weeks, I was waking up with a headache almost every day.

I developed little coughs and colds; the things that I hadn't experienced whilst my body's only focus was to keep me alive!

I obviously suffered major digestive discomfort due to the changing quantity of food I was now eating, often feeling bloated, sick and uncomfortably full.

Of course I was stressed, too, as my normal way of coping with stressful situations was prohibited, and instead of starving myself and exercising, my days were focused on eating and staying still!

At the moment I'm really nervous of gaining weight as my stomach's so full. It may not be comfortable but I know I'm going the right way; this illness will battle me in every sinister way she can but my life is more important. I have the determination to fight for myself, for health and recovery and liberation from this dreadful illness. She has tried to kill me once, and never again will I give her that opportunity.

The dietician looked at my food diary and was pleased with it, but to me it looks like overeating. Then she reassured me by saying that for me at the moment there's no such thing! Any amount of weight I put on is good, the more the better really.

Two packets of Maltesers as a snack made me feel sick and crampy; my stomach has been restless all day. I recognize the tension in my lower back and shoulders, and how the frequency of headaches is increasing, but they say that's due to refeeding.

Woke up soaking in sweat; apparently it's normal during re-feeding. It's actually really strange to finally feel warm and not freezing cold all the time!

I had such an awful stomach last night and was in so much pain that I had to empty myself with a suppository. It was such a relief to get rid of the pain, but I must have emptied myself pretty thoroughly as I had lost weight, and so had my diet upped with an extra supplement drink.

I really want to change from the milkshake supplement drinks to the syrup ones, as I feel like they're giving me awful cramps and make me feel quite sick, especially now I have to have so many every day.

Once again I have a headache – arrrgh! – so I washed my hair: I look like I've walked through a hedge backwards but I don't care! I've got a sore throat too; I've been immune to all little coughs and colds whilst my body was struggling to stay alive when I was at my worst, and now it's not in so much danger I'm getting all the little bugs that most people do, so I guess it's a good sign.

Chapter Six
Mixed Feelings

The dangers of anorexia are extreme, and I often felt I was lectured over and over about the dangers by those who cared about me, just to scare me into getting better. But no amount of fear about the physical effects can make you well again.

However, the striving for a healthy body can be a distraction from the illness, and make weight gain a little more acceptable to the sufferer. For example, I could see the muscle wastage on my body; my scraggly arms and weak legs, but had never applied this same theory to my internal organs; what about my heart? When I began to regain weight in hospital, I felt that with the amount I had been eating, I should have been a lot bigger. This was simply explained to me: the majority of fat had gone into protecting my organs inside.

That helped me to realize how necessary it is to nourish and look after your body by supplying it with the minerals, vitamins it needs.

Competitiveness

Anorexia is an extremely competitive illness, making you fight, not only against others, but even more against yourself. I would constantly push myself to my limits, terrified to seem inadequate, or worse, to fail. People are shocked that I managed to sit my A level exams, let alone pass with flying colours, but that drive to succeed, and the knowledge that anything below 100% was unacceptable, allowed me to keep pushing for my best.

However, my best never impressed the illness, which greedily, always wanted more from me. Every calorie that I cut from my diet, the next day I would have to eat less. The same with exercise; the more I did, the more I would have to do the next day to prevent my anorexia accusing me of being lazy or plaguing me with guilt.

One of the patients described anorexia as being like a drug: it is addictive and you get a high from skipping a meal, from knowing that you are cheating death if you like. One of the therapists described it as a default setting – which we automatically slip into in times of uncertainty or anxiety – that we need to learn to re-programme.

Even once I was in hospital, I found that at one of the most stressful times, mealtimes, there was a shared competition about appearing the most anorexic – nobody wanted to seem the 'greediest' by finishing their plate first, and I still remember the excruciatingly slow pace at which we would eat, eyes darting at other patient's plates to check we weren't speeding too far ahead of everyone else. Everyone was very aware of the dining etiquette and habits of the other patients, even down to the smallest detail such as the angle they held their fork! Despite observing this competition around the table, and hating it, I found myself doing it too, feeling guilty and awkward if I were the first to set down my cutlery.

I'm aware that I eat really slowly here, but I feel like I want to keep to the pace of the table members who also are very slow, then when I'm the slowest I feel panicked and rush to keep up. I don't like people looking or commenting on my food which is why I feel anxious at the table when I see people trying to compare or look. I feel there's a competition to be the slowest! There is a dull atmosphere at the table, superficial and awkward like no one wants to be there in that terrifying situation.

Lunch was pleasant; cottage cheese and salad sandwich

which I ate very quickly compared to everyone else (there is such frustrating competition about being the last to finish eating, I even find myself doing it sometimes!)

Talking to one of the out-patients about how I feel influenced by other patients to eat slower, she identified with how I'm feeling and said she didn't want to finish first and seem like a greedy pig, but over time, she realized that nothing bad came of eating faster than the others, and ate to the speed that she felt comfortable with.

One of the other girls who is leaving soon got anxious that the dietician had told the kitchen to fill her plate right up so as to get her weight up as much as possible before she leaves, and I could see her looking and comparing with my plate, counting how many potatoes there were on both plates!

I feel a competition to eat slower, like I can't have a bite until someone else has had two.

In groups we just talked about the trip to Pizza Express tomorrow, and what behaviours we would challenge; I said mine would be not becoming antisocial and zoned in on my food, and not to be paranoid about the speed that I'm eating at compared to everyone else.

Some of the girls didn't get the drink that they're meant to have with their sandwiches which made me not want mine; why do I have to if they don't? But then that made me worry, what will I be like at home when there's nobody to compare with, and other people may be eating nothing whilst I'm pigging out. I know if I'm having a bad day and there's an opportunity to indulge in anorexic ways then I will.

I'm having a major issue with one of the girls not eating as many snacks as she's supposed to – cutting out here and there and always opting for the lowest cal/fat options.

Perfection

I used to feel so guilty when I ate something that wasn't one hundred per cent delicious and worth every guilty second that followed. I would obsess over the way in which I ate things, in my thoughts fantasizing over each mouthful, and exactly how I would eat it. If it were not the exact food that I wanted, I wouldn't touch it. Anorexia's rules over what I ate were so specific that it became practically impossible to match the demands of the illness.

The anorexia made me very particular in my food choices, and if I were to 'indulge' in a meal and not enjoy it, if that intake of fat and calories wasn't even worth it, I would be punished with a tremendous sense of guilt. This guilt could only be soothed by burning my energy intake with exercise, or further reducing my tiny food intake. Therefore, I became quite uptight about having the 'perfect' snack or meal, and was very indecisive when choosing my menu each morning at The Priory.

Some good advice which I still find myself sticking to nowadays is to opt for the first choice, because obviously this is what you fancy deep down, and if you choose the second and do not enjoy it, you'll always wish you picked the first. Some days I was quite brave, and even asked some of the other patients to choose my snack for me!

Woke up with a headache, thinking frantically about which breakfast cereal to choose and had to consciously occupy my mind with other thoughts. I couldn't decide which jam to have either, got one and then another, and ended up having half and half – not meant to do that, but hey!

I wasn't a perfectionist only about food; I often felt that I had to excel in what I did, and no matter the circumstances, only the best would be acceptable from myself.

When collecting my A level results, I was so pleased and surprised at getting three A grades because I was so ill when I sat them, but at the same time, any other grade would have been a disappointment, so I kind of expected it of myself to get top marks.

I felt so put down and shitty last night; I don't know where I stand any more. I try my hardest and only get criticized for trying to run before I walk, and only the negative aspects get noted. But there shouldn't be negatives! I do expect too much from myself.

Indecision

I still have problems with indecision; the pressure of needing to make the 'perfect choice' often leaves me running away from the options, and not choosing anything at all. But this isn't a way to live life; some decisions have to be made which cannot be run away from, and which will be a lot more important to your future than which type of yoghurt to buy! Which university to go to, what to study, what career path to follow; so many choices yet how do we know which one is the right one?

The truth is that we don't, and through trial and error we discover the people that we are; the tastes that we have, and the personalities that we have developed.

Stick with the first choice you made, as you know in your heart you truly want that.

Snack time was a bit of a wild goose chase between the upstairs and downstairs Starbucks; I was after blueberry cheesecake but they didn't have it, so opted for a yoghurt topped berry swirl but by the time I went to order, the last one had gone! Arrrgh! By this time I was stressed and angry at myself for being so indecisive (a terrible trait of mine that my anorexia has used for its benefit) so I settled for a rocky road and it was surprisingly delish!

It took me so long to decide what crisps to choose. I wrote it in, scribbled it out, and wrote it in again – my indecision is driving me crazy! I had a chat with my co-worker, confessing about my struggle and indecision; was nice to get it off my chest although I always feel like I want to seem like I'm coping and feel like a failure when my actions prove I'm not, so confessing these things is hard for me. Hearing myself say it has made me determined to get back on track tomorrow and get out of my struggle pit which I'm wallowing in.

Being unable to push food away because it wasn't 'perfect' helped me to rationalize, accepting food for fuel rather than always as a pleasure.

I didn't enjoy pudding at lunch, but it was rewarding to eat something that I knew was calorific and wasn't particularly nice but I could eat it knowing I had to, and could laugh about it afterwards.

Dad made my evening snack for me; half cheese sandwich and half Nutella sandwich; it helped me to accept food not perfectly how I want it. Me and Eva had a hot chocolate; an extra which I would normally feel guilty about, but I didn't!

For snack, the therapist and dietician took us to an Italian cafe where I was torn between a custard tart or a chocolate cake, and made the mistake of opting for the chocolate cake – I felt so angry at myself for ploughing through this mound of fat and calories which I didn't even enjoy. On the way back to the hospital I felt tearful yet obsessive, looking at the big, scary world, realizing how strong the anorexia still is inside me.

This evening I avoided having my supplement drink, and when I confessed to another patient, I realized how the illness would simply thrive and grow from this kind of behaviour, and I felt so guilty like I'd cheated the real Ali that I went and got it; I'm so proud that I did that! There is nothing tempting about a supplement drink, except that it is a medicine to help me get better, and having that anorexic reality check in the real world during 'snack out' made me remember how much I want to get better. Lying to myself isn't going to get me better, and self-honesty is the start to any really change.

In CBT [Cognitive Behavioural Therapy] we talked about fear foods, and thinking I had none I was surprised to discover quite a few, like fruit juice, pasta, avocado, bananas and fluid kcals like in smoothies or non-diet soft drinks. My goal is to tackle these fears as the more I do, the less scary they'll become – I don't want the anorexia to decide what foods I can or can't have. When I'm tackling these fears it'll feel horrible because I'm going against the anorexia. If it hurts, recovery is happening!

I tackled fruit juice at lunch, worried about having extra with such a filling meal (baked beans on toast, ginger sponge and custard). I was shaking but did it and didn't feel as bad as I thought I would – in fact it felt great to do it and allow myself juice, being the decider of what I had rather than let the anorexia control me. I felt indecisive when choosing my lunch order, so took my own advice and stuck to my first choice, which I'm glad I did.

This stops me obsessing and regretting afterwards. This also applies to answering exam questions!

Each mouthful is progress

From the day I arrived in hospital, I was ready to use the opportunity to recover, and although it was hard, I made such an effort to comply with the rules, and get on with recovery, feeling that every mouthful would be a step closer to physical recovery, which would help me to be just a bit more prepared for mental recovery. However, recovery is such a slow, painful process I would often become frustrated with myself, wishing that weight gain would alone bring me to complete recovery. I would want to be the perfect patient, compliant and satisfied, whereas in reality it is expected that the illness will kick up a fuss; I was often told by the professionals that if it hurt, it worked.

Although tasty, tea was extremely filling and I polished it off with a heavy pudding; an apple rice pudding. I knew it was a bigger pudding than what would be expected after a larger meal, but I'd rather have something more calorific that I enjoyed than something only OK but lower calorie. I'm trying to get as many calories as I can at the moment, I just seem to have to have a goal for everything. For example, I know I have to eat all of the diet set for me, but try to beat that with as many little extras as I can, like cups of tea, squash or opting for higher calorie snacks. I guess that's good in a way because I'm not allowing the illness to hold me back, not having a limit on anything.

I often felt that by completely changing my environment or my presentation of myself, I would fool myself into being a different person; a person who didn't have my issues. But in reality, it's the person that needs to deal with the issues, rather than escape from them, or bury them down deeper inside. After all, it is the person that changes things, and not the environment.

[Ian] reminded me that recovery cannot be done perfectly; coping with down-days will only make me see how strong I am, and help me to believe in my recovery. He's got me sussed – I seem poised, like everything's fine, but inside I have a volcano of emotions bubbling away under the surface, ready to explode. In a way, I feel that going back to life in Swansea is too anorexic and will be too hard for me; I want to start fresh somewhere else. But one of the patients pointed out that that is my perfectionism, wanting me to crumple up the page of my life, and start all over again.

Black-and-white thinking
The illness dictates very black-and-white thinking: you're either skinny or fat, you either love the meal you

have or don't eat anything at all; therefore if you don't enjoy it one hundred per cent, you have been a greedy pig and not had any enjoyment. And you must suffer for this, trapped in a blanket of guilt.

After depriving myself for years of the 'junk' like Nutella, thick white bread and various puddings, I relished the opportunity to eat anything I wanted. I struggled with eating normal, home-cooked meals like chicken and mash – things that weren't my favourite were simply a waste of calories. For example, I'd rather eat a slightly more calorific chocolate bar, than a boring old bowl of muesli.

Felt very full after tea, but at least I feel less like I'm struggling now – my only problem was the butter at lunch which I made up for with a heavy pudding (although I know it doesn't work like that, the weighing up calories throughout the day, the black-and-white thinking – all very anorexic!).

I feel very extremist with food; either having a huge slab of bread loaded with Nutella, or have nothing at all. I must work on this; it makes me feel so piggish.

In CBT, we talked about all-or-nothing, black-and-white thinking, ie: five course, abundant meal in top restaurant, or nothing at all. I see that getting a balance is so important.

Over time, I came to realize that there is more to a meal; being with people I love in a relaxed environment over flowing conversation contributes to how nice a meal is, and if the food is good, that's a bonus too! I realized too that it's not necessary to love every single meal and snack of the day; what's more important is to fuel your body to fight the illness and to get on with daily activities.

Anxiety

If you are afraid of a certain situation, it is most important that you face it; to be able to recognize that the outcome won't necessarily be the awful prediction that you made. Often, in fact, people comment on how easy it was once they faced their feared situations.

For me, the fear was not the eating in particular, not the passing of each forkful into my mouth, but the terrifying sense of guilt that lay on the empty plate after the food had all been consumed; a feeling of self-revulsion and lack of control that was proved by me having eaten all of my food.

Before I went to hospital, I would just avoid these feelings simply by never eating as much as I should have, never exceeding the allowances that the illness gave me, and if I ever did eat what I though was too much, I would attempt to burn it off through exercise, powered by my infuriation at myself.

As neither exercise nor restriction were possible in hospital, I learnt to work my way through the process, feeling the bad feelings and finding they gradually lessened, as did the terror of having to eat a whole plate of food. And as my recovery progressed, I recognized the benefits that came with defeating the illness.

1.30pm: I feel anxious after lunch of sandwich and crisps and Muller rice, after the dietician told me I had to have another snack mid-afternoon. She asked me how I felt about it and I said OK but I can't help feeling anxious about it – what if I get too overwhelmed? What if I get so panicked I can't deal with it . . . ?!

3pm: I recognized my anxiety increased throughout the day about the extra snack, and that's why I felt tense at lunch. After a while I realized I have to do this to gain weight because I'm not healthy, and the anorexia was making me anxious because I scared it with the concept of pushing it further away and regaining normality without it. Life's a lot better without it because I hate living in fear, and dreading the next mealtime. I HAVE to restore my weight, and stop predicting anxiety; if and when it comes, I should deal with it then. I know I can do it, enjoy the snack and the thought of getting just that little bit nearer normality.

3.45pm: Just after snack, felt really anxious and a bit worked up because I wasn't allowed to dip my Twix bar into my tea and I was told to be careful not to drop crumbs (and lose precious calories!), but I'm glad I've done it, and feel good knowing that I'm that much closer to getting better physically. I hope Dad will see a healthier daughter when he comes to visit me.

Today I have been able to eat and accepted what I've had to eat. I understand why I have to even if I don't particularly like the food, and am gradually feeling less anxious, and when I do start to get worked up I try to consciously relax before mealtimes.

A lot of the time, I find that the actual process of eating the 'scary' meal is not so hard; it's the anxiety building up in your mind beforehand, the anorexic voice poking its opinions in and scaring you for the huge task that is to come. But in such an environment as hospital, where you do not have the opportunity to obey your anorexic voice, once you do it you feel proud afterwards. You feel like shit – like a fat bitch – but at least you have DONE it. You've come that one step closer to being you again. However, being in hospital does not stop the voice from being there; in fact, it just shouts louder as you're rebelling from it so much more. The thoughts still haunt you, the obsession, the body, the horrible cruel darkness of the anorexic world. And the only thing worse than obeying your anorexic voice is disobeying it. And as everyone knows, disobeying means trouble.

I have thought about my feelings and have identified that the thought of weighing 10 stone fills me with dread to the extent that I don't want to recover! By anticipating this, I'm only making myself nervous and the healing process harder. Why think about being almost double my weight when there are so many steps in between?!

I got anxious at lunchtime because I felt that my portion size was too big – it looked huge – and even when the waitress assured me it was the right one for me, I wasn't convinced.

I realize the longer you put something off, the more anxious you'll be about doing it and the best way to become less anxious is to get on and face your fears!

Chapter Seven

Moving On

Initially, I was given six weeks of funding to be an in-patient, yet it was obvious once I was in The Priory that six weeks would not nearly be enough. Even after the three months that, in the end, I was funded for, my consultant felt that I should have had longer, and that I wouldn't fully recover for at least a year. I wanted to get the treatment over and done with and continue life without the illness; if I could have taken a pill to make it go away, I would have, to avoid all the difficulties of having to go through recovery.

At times I felt that I would never get to the places I wanted to go, yet I learnt to be patient with myself, and began to measure my progress in stages of things I was allowed by the nurses, such as being trusted to use the bathroom alone, no longer needing to use the wheelchair, and being able to visit home. The biggest reward was to gain freedom and be getting my own control back. I also began to regain the little things that we take for granted, such as interest in the opposite sex, interest in spending time with friends, and reading.

Distraction

At a stressful moment where the anorexia is fighting against what you know you should do, distraction is a useful tool in focusing your mind on something other than the illness or the discomfort that it inflicts on you.

Enjoyed dinner and find myself anticipating food times, but try not to clock-watch and like to talk about other topics just for a sense of change, and to not feel totally consumed by this illness in every way. I chatted a lot to my key nurse, Alice, and enjoyed sitting with her during dinner whilst she supervised me, but after I'd finished I just wanted to go. I still feel that the days revolve around food, but I try not to worry and work myself up about it; it's the process for physically getting back to the 'Ali' who has been broken down and destroyed by anorexia – will be a tough fight but I'll take it one step at a time, one feeling at a time. Keep positive and motivated, reading over my motivation tips helps a lot.

I'm focusing consciously on anorexic traits and feel a great sense of power when I am able to stop them because I know they'll only hold back my progress and recovery. I feel comfortable about food being so regular, but need to keep myself busy with art, chatting, jewellery-making etc, and hopefully my mind will slowly become less preoccupied by food as I get used to the routine and my body gets used to knowing it will soon be fed.

I'm making a conscious effort to distract my mind from foody thoughts; for example, earlier I found myself wondering what I was going to have for tea, and as I walked down the corridor, began to tell myself really stupid things like, 'That is the doctor, he will prescribe me some ear drops' – anything as long as it's not to do with food! You have to occupy your mind until the temptation to think of food passes.

Breakfast was fine (cereal and two slices of toast) but I hate sitting around afterwards – I need to be busy and keep my mind busy, free from ruminating about how much fat and calories I've just consumed.

I was so very frantic, constantly needing to keep myself busy and occupied, and not allowed to be alone in my room without the supervision of a nurse. I got into the habit of staying in the lounge in the company of the other patients. I was very bored and still felt like the outsider because I wasn't yet participating in the daily activities in group therapies, so didn't know what was going on beyond the small world of the lounge.

I'm going to try and challenge being on my own and comfortable and at peace, not feeling the need to be busy and rush about. The thought of just sitting in peace and quiet terrifies me; how will I cope with having no purpose?

Of course, the aim was for us to recover physically simply by refeeding in a controlled environment, but to pass the long days, and aid the mental healing, we would attend a variety of different therapies. All helped us to distinguish between ourselves and the illness, come to terms with certain aspects of our illness that we had been denying, or simply just to feel less alone; a huge importance of groups for me was to realize that other people had gone through the same suffering that I had. I no longer felt alone.

I really enjoyed taking part for the first time today, finding it really insightful and comforting to know that others have similar feelings, or feel similar worries when thinking about the future as I do.

Groups and therapy

There were certain rules and restrictions for the groups, and the first and foremost was clear: what goes on in groups stays in groups.

It was very intimidating to have to discuss your deepest secrets and most intimate thoughts with a group of people you hardly knew, and to be assured that your secrets would be kept among the group was a relief that made it easier to be honest. When newcomers came to the group, it was often very tempting to hold back and not speak out.

Everyone would eventually be able to attend group, but when you started depended on your weight and your behaviour. You were not permitted to participate at too low a weight as the professionals felt you would be unable to concentrate, therefore wouldn't benefit, or might possibly taint the other patient's attitudes.

When everyone went to drama therapy I sat in the lounge alone as I wasn't allowed to join – apparently my brain wouldn't be able to cope because my illness inhibits clear thinking. I've just done my A levels for God's sake!

After several weeks totally devoted to refeeding, I was given the opportunity to participate in group therapies, which was how we passed the weekdays. Open talking group was for discussing anything from how our weekends went to a small worry on our mind; an opportunity for us to speak individually about anything.

Open talking group was interesting, and I identified with others how we felt it was unnecessary to eat when we weren't exercising, yet by exercising you're only dragging out the illness, making it stronger.

Some therapies helped us to express the real person behind the illness in a more artistic way, such as art therapy, drama therapy or yoga. Drama therapy often involved using a beanbag to represent the anorexia, and we would position it where we felt the anorexia was for us at that time. I liked this because it helped me to distinguish myself from the illness that had consumed me, and consumed my identity.

We had drama therapy where we had to put a beanbag near us to represent where the anorexia was, and I put it on the back of my shoulders to represent how although sometimes I don't see it, it's always there, sometimes so heavy that it's too hard to fight and its heaviness pulls me down. One of the patients mentioned a valid point; how she feels that in hospital she's eating for the nurses, whereas now she's at home more often she is eating for her, and the struggle is a lot harder.

In drama therapy we had to use the beanbag (again!) to represent where we felt the anorexia was (I sat on it to show my get-on-with-it attitude) and where we think others perceive it is with us (on my lap to show it's not always easy to distinguish between me and the illness, which throws people off).

In drama therapy we built a wall and positioned ourselves where we were in relation to the illness; behind or over. I sat on the top, looking out on to the normal world, yet afraid to jump down into the unknown. I'm an onlooker, sad I can't join in and protected by the wall of anorexia. To get to my future I know I need to take risks, but I am not prepared to go back behind the cold, dark lonely place behind the wall.

CBT [Cognitive Behavioural Therapy] involved distinguishing between our thoughts and the feelings that arose in an anxiety provoking situation, as the thoughts are often ignored and the emotions take over, making us avoid the same situation in the future.

It helps to rationalize a situation, and by acknowledging your thoughts, you are able to challenge the feelings, and control the outcome, so that a similar situation in the future does not provoke the same anxiety.

Went to a group where we talked about the vicious cycle of thinking 'I can't eat this, I want control' leading to feelings of panic, self disgust and anxiety which makes us do anorexic behaviours like over-exercise. These give us a momentary high (a rush of adrenaline) which quickly dies, and leaves you feeling isolated, exhausted and trapped. So to get that high again, you must miss another meal, and so it goes on.

Nutritional therapy involved the dietician discussing certain aspects of our diet that were important to us, and what the consequences of cutting out certain food groups could be.

In Nutrition group we talked about how to make a sandwich (rocket science); different types of bread equivalents, alternative fillings etc. – until we all got so excited that a loud discussion over mushy pea toasties and cold bean sandwiches erupted!

After my peanut butter sandwich snack, the dietician brought some bread, pasta and cereal up to the ward, and we all buttered the bread and poured out cereal without measuring it to see if she thought we were doing it right. The thing is, I KNOW how much a normal person should eat cereal-wise, or how thick the spread on their bread should be, but the illness won't let the normal rules apply to me.

In Nutrition group today, I realized I have no idea when I'm hungry or sated or just digesting, because I've ignored the feeling for so long. It will only come back when I've been eating regularly for several months, and reached maintenance weight.

The most helpful group for me was behaviour challenge group, where we identified all the behaviours that the anorexia forced on us, and I discovered the ways in which my illness not only affected me in ways of eating and exercise, but had crept in to infect every aspect of my life in such a sneaky way that I hadn't even noticed. This therapy session helped me particularly in distinguishing a difference between myself and the illness; it's easy to be so consumed by it that you no longer have your own sense of identity.

I am shocked at some of the behaviours anorexics use; things like brushing teeth after meals to get rid of the taste of food, or holding their breath when they walk past food shops so as not to breathe in calories in the smell of food! Some things I do, I didn't even realize were traits, such as filling up on fizzy drinks, using specific cutlery and heating up food to a boiling temperature.

In groups we talked about the importance of not giving up when times are hard and the anorexic option is the easiest. One of the girls described the anorexia as a fire and behaviours as twigs; the more twigs you use, the greater the fire becomes, so the more you use anorexic behaviours, the stronger and more dangerous the illness will become.

For those who had reached a satisfactory weight gain, we were taken out once a week to challenge a particular behaviour or fear, whether it was simply being in the public eye, eating in public, or maybe choosing a fear food as a more challenging snack. Although it was often a very difficult time for many, it was also an opportunity to escape the confinement of the hospital.

I went for an ice cream with two of the other patients at snack time, and got a little worked up as to which ice cream to choose, but when I chose a Malteser ice cream, I was able to enjoy it and without over-focusing on the food aspect of the trip; I watched the people walking around, felt the warmth of the sun and the freedom of being in the open air, and heard the soothing sounds of the waterfall nearby. I really enjoyed myself and didn't feel anxious or guilty which I was chuffed about.

My challenge in Broadmead was to eat a snack surrounded by people who weren't eating, so I wandered to the other side of the shopping centre with a white chocolate cookie in one hand and a supplement drink in the other. I noticed a few people looking (one man trying to catch my eye who smiled at me) and a few people that I guess just looked at me like I was looking at them, just passively without bothering to develop an opinion. I enjoyed the cookie, and was more occupied with that than noticing shame or feeling conscious. We briefly discussed how everyone's outing went; surprisingly better than expected for most!

One-to-one sessions, both with our psychiatrists and with therapists, were also very helpful as they would be more focused on our individual issues, and we could open up in ways that we felt we couldn't in a group situation.

We could also work with a ward nurse on a 'log book' which asked us questions about our illness, to find routes or triggers, and this was the initial stage of our Stage Work.

I worked through my log book with my key nurse, which helped me to see my anorexia as a shield against being bullied; no one will feel I'm a threat if I look as pathetic and feeble as I do now!

We were all asked to do Stage Work, which involved answering a series of questions about our personal experiences of our illnesses to gain insight into it. The third stage was to read our life story, which I discovered was surprisingly intimidating, and despite wanting to conceal particular stories that displayed my weaknesses, I discovered my true feelings about certain events in my life which prior to reading it out, I had held in.

I completed my first Stage Work, where I was able to see how my anorexia gives me a sense of achievement. One of the therapists told me my piece was very powerful.

Some of the other patients seemed to be smirking at me as I worked on my Stage Work so soon after finishing my first part, but I don't care, I feel this helps me with my recovery and at the end of the day, the only reason I'm here is for me!

In my Stage Work, something powerful that a therapist

thought I said was that you can't be a little bit anorexic –
either you live your life or the illness does.

I found one of the therapist's sessions especially
motivating and insightful. She described anorexia as a
child who is having a tantrum and the mother is giving
in by giving it what it wants to make it be quiet, but if
she continues this behaviour, rewarding its bad
behaviour with what it wants, it will learn that this is
how to get its way. However, if the mother persists in
staying strong, doing what she knows is right and not
giving in to the demands of the child, although it will
be difficult and seem easier to just give in, the child will
eventually realize that it won't get its way and the
tantrum dies; the mother wins.

Ward round

Wednesday afternoons would transport me back to the
days of being a schoolchild waiting for the comments
on a school report; waiting for the terrifying moment
in which you'd discover the truth, from which came
the consequences. An intimidating yet important
experience, 'ward round' was the only opportunity to
make requests in front of my consultant, my dietician,
therapists, doctor, charge nurse and key nurse. It was
the place that I got answers, and a response to my

progress, and where they could give you more allowances, or even increase your diet.

In ward round they increased my diet to three supplement drinks and two snacks; overwhelmed me and I felt very unhappy about having to eat more. Felt like saying, ' No thank you!' but I'll do it, think of it like medicine. They said that my weight gain wasn't satisfactory, and although my consultant wants me to come off all supervision, the charge nurse thought it should be a slower, more gradual process. But luckily, I'm allowed to eat with my family – yay!

Also, the therapists said I was really co-operative and well-focused in groups, but I'm not yet able to come on the behaviour trips out because my weight is still too low. I can't help feeling nervous about all of those supplement drinks I now have to have; will I manage three a day?! But I want to try it to show myself I can; I believe that I can recover and learn to love the person that is hiding inside.

In ward round everything went well, apparently I'm contributing well in groups, the dietician actually said I'm doing well, and should focus on today, rather than worry about things in the future which may not even happen. So pleased that I'm able to go home for three nights; that's long for a first weekend home but I'm determined to do well. I owe it to myself not to muck this weekend up; it will only make me more anxious about going home permanently.

Bingeing

I came to realize the false sense of control I had had about my eating habits, and after being so out of control in my eating for so long, and finally being re-introduced to food, I felt myself very panicked and often thinking about bingeing. We were all warned about the high risk of bingeing once an anorexic begins to refeed in a non-controlled environment, and that anorexia can easily develop into Bulimia; I was terrified of extending my illness.

Food was such an emphasis that I felt that my life was a constant cycle revolving around it: eating, waiting for meals as something to do in the days rather than sit around, and then sitting about feeling full! Yet I still thought obsessively about food, often dreaming about it, and when I was on my first weekend home, I felt it necessary to plan all the wonderful things I wanted to enjoy.

I woke up obsessively thinking about what I could eat on my day home on Thursday, but hopefully talking about it and having it in black and white on a food plan will make things easier. It's the first day in a long time that I will be able to eat what, and as, I please, without being limited by the hospital menu or my illness. I want to indulge in all the wonderful foods I adore and have been deprived of for so long!

I can't express the sheer terror the thought of a binge still brings to me even now, and even if I eat a lot more than I would normally, I still have to rationalize by comparing to how much other people eat to see if it's a normal amount.

I passed a lot of time doing art, yet I still found myself anticipating mealtimes, feeling like I was waiting for meals and even once I ate and was full, my thoughts would still go to food, and that if I could binge then I probably would.

I'm feeling nervous about how I would cope in the real world, because I don't feel I would have the ability to control myself around food. They say that the more starved you are, the more likely you are to binge. Why am I thinking so much about food?! I get annoyed with myself about this, I feel like my day is structured around food and mealtimes and it is overwhelming, yet I overwhelm myself more with these constant thoughts of food and when is the next meal. Anorexia is not a person, nor a feeling nor a purpose, and I won't allow myself to be broken down by it any more.

I have a pain down the right side of my body from stress, but what hurts me the most is being uncomfortable in this body, the ache of wanting to get out.

I feel so guilty from the weekend just gone, of trying to 'live it up' in London and eating the types of food I rarely eat. I waste away the calm before the storm, anticipating the hard times that will inevitably follow the good. When will what I consider a binge become just an overeat, like it is for most other people? Why are there different rules for me? Am I always going to have to feel panic and self-disgust when I eat a normal/large meal, spend the next few days having to starve myself to 'undo' the bad work. I didn't want to stop eating, as I knew that once I admitted defeat, and politely thanked the waitress for clearing away my empty plate, the feelings would soon come seeping in, and I would be left with the sharp stone sitting heavily in my stomach, reminding me and punishing me for my unacceptable behaviour.

All day, I've eaten: a slice of chocolate cake, two chocolates and a chicken and brie burger from GBK. I am so disgusted and ashamed to admit it, all I want is for people to tell me, 'It's not that much' because that means the anorexia still differentiates me; I'm not one of those run-of-the-mill lard arses. I'm on safe ground when people say, 'You ate the smallest portion' or 'You didn't eat very much', or even when other people seem to eat a huge amount more than me, but when even my well-fed brother comments that he's impressed with how much I managed – 'After all, it was huge!' – that's when the panic creeps in; my anorexia is cornered and embarrassed. And it doesn't like it, so I pay for it for the next few days until the pain subsides.

How I feel right now is indescribable; dirty, revolting, out-of-control. I can't trust myself with food any more; I'm so scared to binge, so sick of my 'all or nothing' thinking which will only get me to the other end of the spectrum concerning eating disorders. I will be fat, but still feel this pain – will I ever win?! Will I ever settle for a simple ham sandwich, or will it either be a lunch of a glass of water and an apple, or a door wedge cheese and bacon burger with all the greasy trimmings? All I need is balance, and that's the one thing that the illness is not letting me enjoy at the moment.

Control

Although I have always been very close to my mother, there was a tension which is common between a teenager embarking on adulthood and their mother. It is impossible to have two females at the head of the household. My need to retain control over myself, and refuse her control, was expressed through my anorexia.

I allowed her no control over my eating habits; rejecting her cooking, avoiding eating with her as I would feel ashamed when she saw me eat, falling into a blind rage when she went food shopping without me.

On occasions such as the latter, my anorexia would panic at the sight of the vast selection of delicious new products, causing me to make everyone fully aware of how it was wrong in some way or another, as through my anorexia's eyes, she was trying to fatten me up by supplying the temptations that she knew I loved. She was trying to take away my control. I preferred the cupboards to be empty, tidy, free of temptation.

I got back and began to prepare a sandwich, which mentally I had planned for myself, and Mum began to challenge me; why was I preparing a sandwich when she'd already made dinner? She plonked a plate of salmon, potatoes, carrots and peas with some mango salsa in front of me, and I just could not eat it. She kept pushing, saying things like 'Start eating!' and 'I hope you don't behave like this in hospital'.

I wanted to throw the plate across the room, I felt so angry about wasting my calories on it. There was an awkward vibe after that, and I felt humiliated in front of my nephew who must have been thinking how childish I was to burst into tears over a plate of food. I was frustrated with Mum, who kept blaming herself: 'Did I serve the wrong food?', 'Why is it so hard for you to eat my cooking?' I was so angry I felt as if it would tear my stomach to pieces, I cried and cried, angry at everything.

Mum took me and Tom to the cinema to see 'Evan Almighty'; was a laugh and something to occupy my mind, and was able to eat a little something to make up for the missed meal at lunch. Mum attempted to make food for tea for me, but I wish she'd just leave me to do it myself! I just wanted to go back to the hospital then, feeling relieved to get back on the train, sick of the awkward atmosphere.

I chatted to my doctor who'd had a worrying phone call from my mum over how the weekend went badly. I'm so angry at her that I don't want to speak to her, but I have to discuss the fact that I have only fifteen days more funding in my safety haven of hospital, especially as the specialists are worried too. We talked about how the anorexia may be a way of rebelling and taking control, explaining why I'm so against eating Mum's cooking and get so irritated by Mum interfering in my business where food is concerned. Food is my way of getting control from my mother.

I found a similarity with one of the other patients when she told me how angry she would get if her mother came into the kitchen whilst she was trying to prepare a meal, because she wanted the control, and wanted to be able to do it herself, something I experienced with my own mother.

I felt very anxious in the presence of my mum, not wanting her to sit with me whilst I ate and feeling irritated when she asked me why I was diluting my milk with water (I said nothing and quickly changed the subject, when I should have told the truth – I'm a slave to my illness!).

Looking back, I can now see how deluded I was in feeling I'd achieved control from this self-destructive way of being. My illness would have to be reassured that it was in control in various ways. I would have to feel hungry, leave a little on my plate, as if to prove I could hold back from eating if I wanted to.

I know how many calories I need to gain weight, so that is a quantifiable goal, but there's no necessary amount of fat or consequences to cutting it out, except for giving the anorexia a sense of control.

Got worried I'd overdone it and threw the last scraps in the bin; it's like I need there to be a little left on my plate so the anorexia feels in control.

The best thing I got from the illness was a sense of control, but now I can be in REAL control by becoming the person I want to be. By making mistakes and taking risks (stepping out of your comfort zone) you learn the most important lessons of life.

Losing the obsession

In my original diary, I talk incessantly about food, but I can't begin to explain how food is your only thought, only field of interest. It haunts you constantly, and you will jump at any opportunity to involve yourself with food, like cooking, reading up on recipes, watching cooking programmes and wandering the aisles of a supermarket, just to tease yourself. To be aware of all the wonderful things available and to see how strong you are being by resisting temptation, whereas in reality it proves how strong the illness is holding you in its clutches. I even recall a dream so vivid of eating breakfast that when I woke up, I truly believed that I'd already had it!

During my session with my consultant, she told me that the reason that I think about food so much is because my body is telling me to eat; it's a starvation prevention as your body reminds you how desperate you are to get food. She said if a dog is starved, it is as restless as we are – hungry dogs never rest – explaining my abundance of energy even at my lowest and most emaciated weight. In fact, the hungrier I am, the less able I am to relax.

I had a good, long chat with my doctor who told me I was being very honest (I'm glad she said that because I feel like I haven't been) and she drew me something to help me understand 'my drive to search for food'. As I slowly get to a healthier BMI, my thoughts and preoccupation with food have lessened. The hungrier I am and the lower my food intake, the more the body desperately tries to get fed, and this involves filling the brain with thoughts of food.

I thought a lot about food in hospital, feeling that as soon as I'd finished one meal, I'd be wasting time until the next meal. Food was the only thing to 'do' around there, and any other little thing was simply a distraction from the never ending food supply that we knew was coming.

I feel overwhelmed by the consistent obsessional thoughts of food that dominate my mind, clouding over any rational or normal thoughts a teenage girl should be having. I know it's not normal what is going through my head, and feel ashamed and disgusted with my abnormal thinking.

I had a very foody dream about all the chocolate bars I could have as a snack, I feel quite panicked by the wider choice of things in the 'real world', something I have to face when going back home.

I felt quite obsessive today with the amount of food and anticipation for the next meal. Why do people eat when they're bored?! It does feel like a constant reel of food; quite overwhelming.

Reflecting back on today, I feel pleased with myself for fighting obsessional food thoughts, not allowing myself to get into an indecisive state by sticking to my first choice, and not analyzing the choice; I'm definitely on my way out of the struggle rut.

Over time I began to see the anorexic obsession with food in other newcomers. New patients in denial of their illness used the same traits that I used to.

I felt proud of myself for having got on and eaten

everything asked of me, whilst one of the other patients was refusing to eat her snack and drawing attention to how disgusting she felt about overeating to such an extent. Although I can relate to what she's saying and identify it in feelings I've had before, I won't let other people's issues slow down my recovery. When I attempted to reassure her by pointing out that in calorific terms, I was eating double the amount she was, she dismissed it by saying, 'But you're so thin, you're allowed to'. We're all in the same boat, and you've just got to fight against all the rules and routines that you've been forced into for so long by your illness.

The latest scandal is that one of the new girls has been stuffing food in her socks, and then chucking it out of the window – twisted what the illness can do to you.

A new girl came in today, and seeing how tough it is for her made me realize how far I've come in the little time I've been here; chatting to her and motivating her motivates myself, reminds me of the reasons that I'm complying with getting better, and rebelling against the illness.

This morning I found it really difficult to hear one of the girls talk in such an anorexic way; she was begging the nurses to 'make it stop, make it go away' when she told them she just couldn't drink a supplement drink.

This evening I missed my supplement drink; I KNOW it's the anorexia but I seem to try and push the boundaries and see how far I can get away with it. I hate seeing other patients hiding and chucking out their snacks when the nurses think they have eaten it, but although it disturbs me, I can fully understand doing it myself. It's the illness seeing how far it can push and get away with it.

Something extremely difficult for both the sufferer and their carers is the inconsistency of the illness. One day you can feel on top of the world, proud of how you are, inch by inch, slowly becoming the person that is truly you by challenging the anorexia, and the next you can be driven to obey your anorexia without even being aware of it. The most important thing is to acknowledge your mistakes, even if someone else has to point them out to you, and remember it's acceptable to make mistakes; what matters is what you do to amend them.

Self-awareness can get you very far, as long as you remember to act on it. You are the one who has control. Sometimes, something as simple as having a cup of tea seems so difficult that I just have to have one to prove to myself how easy it is, and how good it feels to be the one deciding not to obey the illness. It's a slow and painful process, and it can feel like you're trying to walk up a downward escalator; that the effort is greater trouble than it's worth especially when you don't appear to be getting anywhere.

But recovery will be 'three steps forward, two steps back', and a critical eye often only sees the things you could have done better, rather than admiring all the little achievements. Some great advice that I received was to list all the little things that I've achieved in one day that would have been impossible several months ago.

A lot of my anorexic behaviours have lessened whilst being in hospital, but there are some very difficult, dominating ones that I want to tackle, like indecision, fantasizing over food, body checking, and delaying eating mixed with prolonging the process of eating by eating slowly. Eating is the pleasure that I have banned and restricted myself from for so long, that I want to enjoy it as much as I can.

I thought a lot about going back, to restricting, exercising and finding reassurance in the behaviours I've been deprived of; it's so easy to slip back into it's scary.

Not doing certain behaviours still upsets me, making me feel frustrated and panicked, but I need to stick by this feeling, feeling how the illness makes me feel when I'm not obeying it, and thinking about how every minute of my day was consumed by these strict, endless rules.

Accepting help

In group therapy, I asked what did it mean when someone said that you were struggling. The response was that when you think you're strongest, you're probably struggling, and it's difficult to spot yourself; it's often a case of relying on others to tell you! After I spoke, I burst into tears, but it was such a relief for me to get that off my chest as it had been playing on my mind and getting me down all weekend. It's so good to talk; I felt a great sense of support earlier from other patients.

On one hand I wish people would deal with their own problems and not interfere with others, but at the same time it's easier for others to identify your anorexic behaviours and to make you aware of them, so that you can start to challenge them.

Me and one of the other girls had a nice chat over dinner, then I watched her go on an anorexic walk, refusing to let the anorexia take ME on a walk. I will fight it!

I told one of the girls I couldn't go for a walk in the morning as I knew I'd go for one later – good Ali fighting the baddy!

I'm conscious of the anorexic traits I'm forced into doing by my illness, pushing me to burn a few more calories, and I'm trying desperately to break the habits. Dad helped to motivate me earlier; reminding me anorexia is not a friend, but a thieving enemy.

I counted how many times I body checked in twenty-four hours, and was horrified to discover that I did it nineteen times!

Emotions

Having a positive mindset is absolutely crucial in recovery, to believe that even if life itself isn't better when you are recovered, at least you are the capable YOU again to make your life as good as possible.

Feeling positive and ready to get back – I love being in a motivated mood and feeling strong to fight the illness because it feels a lot easier to battle it this way.

Today my depressed mood seems to have lifted, or is definitely easing, as I am remembering what I'm fighting for.

Everyone needs a certain sense of control in some aspect of their life, and my anorexia had become my way of control. Despite wanting to recover, I had relied on the illness to guide me for so long that it was all I had come to know, and the thought of leaving it terrified me, and made me frustrated with those who were taking it away from me. I was also frustrated by the fact that people forgot the girl inside me, and treated me simply as a victim of anorexia, who couldn't be trusted.

I feel like I'm slowly beginning to succeed in this mental battle; always trying to think positively but nothing seems to be happening; everything is always 'no', and I feel stuck in the same place as when I arrived. Still in the wheelchair, still have my bathroom locked, still under full supervision, still anorexic. I dream of being back home, but then I get scared of how life would slip back to anorexia despite the progress I've made being an in-patient so far. At the moment, I feel so frustrated because I feel walked over, I'm the new girl that doesn't know all of the rules, and hate how people who think they have authority try to bully me.

I felt so miserable for no apparent reason; just frustration due to lack of control tempts me to use anorexic behaviour, then I feel guilty for being tempted because the sane girl in me knows how wrong and damaging they are. Mum is worried about me; she thinks I'm depressed, as does the doctor who came to chat with me, and I think I'm just impatient and enjoy wallowing in my self pity, and dramatizing things.

I've had enough of that stupid word anorexia – ENOUGH! No one is listening to me, how much I need to get away, get on with life. I'm so frustrated and angry and fed up of feeling so full and fat and greedy on these cakes and chocolates, I feel I will literally explode out of my clothes!

I constantly feel sick, angry and low. I'm furious that people see me as struggling, and don't understand how the speed that I eat things means that I'm finding it difficult. Surely if I were to wolf it down and swallow my food whole, I would be accused of trying not to taste it!

Imagine a balloon that is being filled with water. The balloon slowly swells, and only the effects of the liquid inside it are obvious; the water itself remains invisible. However, over time, the balloon reaches its limit, and it explodes, allowing all the stored up water to come spilling out. It's the same with emotions that are pent up by the illness. I became quite emotionless at the most severe stages of my illness, passive and quite unfazed. The emotion – any pain or anger – became buried under my illness, and ignored. So in hospital, as the real me warmed up, and the anorexia began to melt away bit by bit, only then did the feelings begin to pour out.

My doctor wanted to prescribe me some drugs to calm me; I said I wasn't fussed, thank you! I felt very emotional after talking to her, trying to fight back tears all day. My throat welled up so many times I thought it might explode!

I don't feel like talking at the moment, having this anger bubbling up inside of me that I don't know how to get rid of. I feel like crying, and eating is taking me a lot longer.

Couldn't sleep last night, and woke up with swollen, puffy eyes from all that crying yesterday.

I feel so down and have a pain in my stomach – once again! My parents came down earlier and although I love seeing them, there's nothing to do and I feel frustrated. I feel like isolating myself and have an overwhelming urge to burst into tears at any moment.

During the worst stages of my illness, I felt divorced from any emotion, as if it was all building up inside. Yet by embarking on recovery, the bottled-up emotions began to rise to the surface, and I often found myself on the verge of tears; moods swinging from high optimism and enthusiasm for a future without anorexia, to feeling down and depressed; terrified of the changes and uncertainties that I would have to face now I was no longer protected by the anorexia.

I also became very angry; sometimes it was the frustration of the illness being unable to do what it liked, and other times it was simply my emotion, which I was not used to feeling or showing. I was encouraged to let the feelings out, and although it felt weak to cry in front of others, I came to see that storing these emotions and pushing them down inside only has detrimental effects on yourself.

In anger management sessions, I realized how I bottle up my emotions then take it out on someone close to me like my mum. Homework was to write down angry situations this week – they're so frequent it shouldn't be hard to think of something! I get frustrated quite a lot lately, feeling trapped not only in hospital, but inside the illness as well.

Therapist told me that it is normal to feel worse as you recover, as you are becoming more aware of your feelings, which you have been numb to for so long. The illness doesn't let you feel, and acts like a barrier between any human feelings.

I felt teary after lunch, and ashamed for revealing how weak I am, but people said they've never seen me cry and it was nice to see the true me. I realize I bottle up my feelings because I want others to see me as strong and inspirational. Talking to one of the therapists, he said I need to come out from behind this poised, perfect mask and allow myself to moan when things are tough, and be honest with myself.

It's essential to alleviate stress and allow yourself to relax, whether it be with yoga, meditation, or simply listening to relaxing music alone.

It is useful to extract yourself from the stressful situation, and allow the difficult emotions to pass whilst you're distracted.

It is easier to think about the situation in a more rational way, once you can identify your emotions and the reasons for them.

Metacognition involves looking on and analyzing a situation from that of a third person, helping you to see an unbiased viewpoint and recognize behaviour patterns.

For example, by doing this I was able to see how I took my frustrations out on my mum because I knew that no matter how brattish I was to her, she would love me unconditionally no matter how unstable I was feeling. (The illness enjoyed this as it was pushing away a strong source of support that helped me constantly throughout my recovery.)

Was a shitty food day, and Mum came for lunch with me, but I didn't say a word to her. I felt angry that she could be relieved about the news I found so hard, and when she asked me to talk to release my anxieties, I just couldn't. But after, we went into the garden, and I just cried and cried – couldn't stop and all of this anger and frustration and hatred towards the illness came pouring out. And it felt fantastic.

The illness made me into such a selfish person, wanting things my illness's way and getting extremely angry if something was out of place. I felt so frustrated, locked up by my illness, and angry when my mum obeyed the instructions of the hospital to not walk around when they took me out. I remember giving her silent treatment after she asked a guard to let her drive the car right next to where we were going, rather than in the normal car park which would involve walking.

Mum is so pushy about how much I walk when we go out, I know she's only trying to comply with the hospital rules but it makes me so angry; why do I bother going out with them if it's just like being in hospital all the time?! I demanded to be taken back to the hospital rather than stay at my aunt's house, and I could see how stressed my dad got when he's normally so laid back; he went home early and I could see how people were discussing me on the hush, trying to act normal when the atmosphere was so awkward. I felt so guilty and apologized to everyone for my childish, selfish behaviour, but they were all understanding, and once again, I was allowed to be like that because I'm ill.

I rang Mum later to say thank you for being so lovely when I was such a bitch, and although she offered to come up, I felt I needed some space and spent the evening making jewellery.

I feel guilty about the way I pushed Mum and Dad away yesterday with my moody behaviour, so sent them an apology letter reminding them how much I do care for them, and the reason that I'm taking my frustrations out on them is because I trust them.

This evening I met up with Cat for a meal, and Mum demanded that she drive me up the hill to her house (literally a two-minute walk!), threatening to take me back to The Priory if I walked, which made me furious. I'm so angry at her, what's the point in me coming home if it's still like I'm in hospital?

Mum's really annoying me by being really strict and enforcing the rules; I'm so pissed off with her but don't want to make it hard for her, but I feel like she's making it hard for me.

Chapter Eight
Self-Esteem

Everyone understands that the person with the illness suffers huge amounts, but you can't forget those around you who suffer too. To this day I feel terrible for the nightmare I pulled my parents into, for the scraggly mess my friends had to hang around with. It didn't just consume me, but it brought those around me into the same pit of despair.

The illness punishes you by making you feel very alone; it's important to allow yourself to talk to others. Often simple human contact can help to offload, encourage, or feel consoled. Remember that this illness blinds the sufferer, distorting reality, and it takes a second opinion to help to see what is really there. One of the telltale signs that someone is feeling low is that they huddle into themselves, not accepting the love or comfort of another person.

I feel so down for no reason, it's so much easier when the day starts as a positive one. I'm sick and tired of this stupid illness, sick of feeling like everyday I have to be one hundred per cent positive when inside I feel at rock bottom. I've strived so hard to lose all this weight, and now I'm in such a mess I have to throw down huge amounts of food that I don't particularly want, just to gain weight!

I recognize the reason that I have improved already is that I'm ready to live without the illness, and am able to fight it, if it's broken down into manageable steps. This is a technique most people use for everyday challenges, and although I may have to sacrifice things like thinness, I know I will reap the benefits of normality later on. I need to stay focused, stay positive and take things slowly. Predicting anxiety will only make recovery seem so much more impossible than it really is.

My anorexia took all of my self-esteem from me, making it impossible to take a compliment positively. However, as my physical recovery became more apparent, and people began to make positive comments, I was able to take these comments as people's way of noticing 'Ali' coming back, their way of encouraging me throughout my ongoing, torturous battle with the unwelcome voice inside.

When people simply point out how much 'bigger'

you look, it can feel like an insult. But that's your illness on a bad day, flaring up and punishing you for receiving such a compliment.

Anorexia is not about size, weight or food; it's about self-hate, punishment and low self-esteem. It's about hating yourself so much, being so ashamed of what you are, that you reach the desperate measures of self destruction that make you feel anything but yourself.

I found a gorgeous bob on the internet, which I took to the hairdresser, pointed to and said, 'That one please!' I was a little nervous of such a drastic change, and could see my long locks piling up on the floor, the weight on my head getting lighter and lighter, but when it was finished, I was so pleased with the end result, and felt like I had pampered myself, something I haven't bothered to do for a long time. Who would be looking at me anyway, except for a gawp at how scraggly and skinny I looked. There has been a change in me, and I wanted to make that physically apparent. I went into town, and tried on a few things but didn't buy. I'm still in that stage where I can buy plentifully for others, but don't have enough self worth to buy for myself.

Compliments

Unlike a lot of anorexics, I knew that I was scarily underweight, and I understood why people would look at me with horror: why on earth would anyone do that to themselves? And the answer is, they wouldn't. This was the outcome of what was going on inside my mind, and not the objective of the illness. The illness wanted to take everything away from me, and taking my physical health was just one of the many things it very nearly permanently destroyed.

I often found it very positive when people told me how much 'better' I was looking because I knew that what they were saying was right. Although I knew it meant 'bigger', that was a good thing too, because bigger is exactly what I needed to be.

I feel anxious that once I've left my anorexic body and people see me as a normal size, they will expect me to be normal and I will be messed up in my mind but with no apparent protection.

I caught sight of how much I weighed when I first came in, and it is so inhumanly light; all I think is that I'm so lucky to be alive, and never want to go back to that ever again.

One of the night-nurses popped her head around the door and commented on how much better I was looking since she last saw me, which helped to motivate me and I felt like I was getting somewhere.

I chatted to one of the therapists whilst other girls dispersed shopping, and she told me my efforts are noticeable in my appearance; I'm taking more care of myself. Even walking through lower court, one of the nurses did a double take and said, 'You're looking well!' It's brilliant to feel improvement and to know my efforts are appreciated. It's been so long since I've been complimented for looking so good!

I dressed up to go out with the girls and when I got to my friend's house, her grandma kept saying how good I looked; how before my face was like a mask and now I'm 'Ali' again – it felt really nice for people to care that I was better.

An old friend and her mother came round, and kept saying how well I looked; a great ego-booster and shows that my progress is apparent. You can take that kind of comment as an insult, but it's only insulting your illness, and congratulating the real you on becoming stronger; by taking it as a compliment, you can get back the self-esteem that you need.

During the more severe stages of my illness, I neither attracted any male attention, nor was I interested in it; the thought of it actually repulsed me. However, as my recovery became physically apparent, and I gained a natural, healthy glow, I found the increase in male attention difficult to deal with, and couldn't understand that men looked at me because they found me attractive; I believed they were still looking at my anorexia.

Night out, it was nice to have a good dance, but I couldn't handle male attention as leery boys attempted to come on to me, making me feel shy and awkward. I'm not used to it; it's been three months since I last went out!

Mum and Dad came slightly before snack time, so instead of having the peanuts that I ordered, I spotted a ninety-nine ice cream van (yuuuuum!!!) and hopped out of the car, in the pouring rain for an ice cream! We drove to a pub where we sat with drinks and chatted, although I felt conscious of men staring; I felt angry, like saying 'Is there something on my face or something?!'

Self credit

It is extremely easy to stray from the exercise or diet plan for a healthy body and mind in such small gradual stages that it hardly seems there has been any change at all, and only looking back is it obvious how the illness is gradually taking back control. Although setbacks and lapses are normal, I would feel angry at myself for giving into anorexic ways, and allowing my illness to snatch back a bit of control, but it's important to pick yourself back up and press on with recovery; a lapse doesn't necessarily mean a relapse.

I feel like I can't participate in groups properly at the moment, like whenever I give my opinion someone talks over me or disregards what I say. I find I want to hold back what I say because I hate hearing me talk about myself but then again I don't want to talk for anyone else, the only experience I have is my own.

In recovery it is easy to put yourself down and look at the negative aspects, where you could have improved, and focus on things you didn't do, rather than pat yourself on the back for the small things you did achieve. The illness is very inconsistent, and as recovery is 'three steps forward, two steps back', it feels like you're often not getting anywhere. But over time, you realize that there is a gradual improvement.

This week my behaviour challenge is to stick to my food

plan, but not beat myself up if I muck up, and don't give up if things go wrong. I vow to myself to be more honest when the anorexia has gotten its way concerning food choices.

Patience equals progress

After weigh-in and an ECG, it was confirmed that I no longer had to use the wheelchair – YAYYYY!!! I can't express what a relief it is and it marks me having reached sixty per cent of my ideal weight. I'm so pleased that my air mattress has been taken away and a normal one replaced – it's so much more pleasant (and quieter) to be in my room! One of the therapists came to ask if I wanted to have my snack out tomorrow afternoon; I'm so excited to do that as I feel like it's another mark of progress going out into the big, wide world and choosing something that hasn't been calorifically monitored.

I have made small advancements like having my toilet door unlocked and only being supervised during and after meals and snacks as opposed to 24/7 – they are rewarding and showing me that I'm doing well and moving on.

Today I had my first unsupervised snack, but still sat at the snack table with everyone anyway; it felt good to know that they trust me just that little bit more, and I want to prove that I'm trustworthy. In ward round I was taken off all supervision, and am allowed to have a snack out on the weekend with my family! I'm also allowed to go home to pick up my A level results this month; they told me they'd have to trust me.

When I went for a drive with Nicky, I realized the extent of how thin I still am although I have put on a lot, but I will keep plodding on, step by step! I came back in time for snack, munching on Maltesers in front of the telly; something I wouldn't have dreamt of doing a few weeks ago!

My consultant seemed pleased with me; I think now she understands I genuinely want to get better. I feel very motivated at the moment, and happy to gain weight because I want to get better SO MUCH. When I reach my goal the outcome will be phenomenal. But I must learn to be patient and look at the progress I've already made to encourage me.

After being allowed one unsupervised meal tomorrow, I chose breakfast, and as my parents will be here I can eat lunch and dinner with them! Wednesday I am allowed two unsupervised meals, so there is gradual progress! I will talk to my doctor at a later date about whether I can go out on the weekend with my parents, I do hope I can! At *seventy-five per cent of my required weight, I am allowed one ten minute walk, and although I'm not far off, I'm not there yet. I feel very pleased about all of these changes, a real turnaround from a shitty weekend.*

My neighbour, Moira, popped around too, to say how well I looked, and how I was getting my spark and attractiveness back.

When one of the girls said she felt low yesterday, I told her that every low day means a high day, and every high day gradually gets higher and higher until you see a small light at the end of the tunnel, you seem a little stronger than the illness, and can see that there is a possibility of a life without anorexia.

So nervous to get weighed as I knew if I didn't gain I would have my diet increased. I asked the charge nurse to say 'yes' if I could have a walk and she didn't – I was gutted and terrified that would mean six snacks! I ploughed my way through Bran Flakes and raspberry jam toast after panicking and cancelling my bowl of porridge. But then I came up and was told 'oh, yes, you can have a walk!' – I was so relieved I could have jumped up and hugged her! I had my first walk; so exhilarating to chat and be able to move my feet!

It's great to be able to read again; to concentrate all the way through a book and actually take in what it says! It talked about sexual flings and I realized how much I missed that. I went to the cinema with my aunt to see 'The Bourne Ultimatum'; brilliantly action packed with hunky men running around! Pleased to be able to sit through and concentrate on a film too!

I'm feeling really high in spirits and positive about the changes happening to me. I'm able to see myself as 'Ali', not an ill girl, and I love having my identity back!

Like any long-term illness, anorexia doesn't just pack up and leave when you decide you want to get better. It frustrated me so much when I would struggle with the things I thought I could tick off the 'to-do' list, and when things that I could do at the beginning of the week now seemed an impossibility.

I thought that once the weight was on, and people no longer saw the illness in me, that I would be recovered. But professional experts estimate that it takes a year at your maintenance weight (a BMI of 20 or above) to recover fully.

It's important to remember to be patient with yourself, and take each day as it comes; it will eventually get easier. On average, it takes about five years for the anorexia's powerful voice to completely fade; many feel that they are still haunted by its taunts, but they become much fainter, and easier to ignore with increasing strength.

Anorexia is the mental illness with the highest mortality rate, killing twenty per cent of its sufferers, who either starve to death or commit suicide to escape the world of pain that the illness has immersed them in. These statistics would not be so scary if we could click our fingers and suddenly feel better; suddenly be able to ignore the thing that has torn our lives apart! It wouldn't be such a big deal if we could simply turn around and 'decide' not to be ill any more.

It was a shock to see the pictures of me when I was at my lowest weight, my skin pulled across my bones like cling film, the tops of my legs the size of my wrists. It repulsed me and reassured me that weight gain is such a good thing; if I ever feel tempted to lose weight, those pictures will be enough to remind me what a hell I lived in, if you can call it living.

I'm shocked at the thinness of one of the new girls, and it scares me; I never want to go back to my lowest weight; nothing could ever tempt me to go back to that hellhole.

It is essential to remember that you cannot be a little bit anorexic; it's the illness or you that wins this game. This is an ugly, thieving illness, that is never satisfied until it has taken everything, including your existence. Remind yourself of how difficult times were at rock bottom; is that really how you want to live your life? Look at the benefits of recovery, and how far you've come and how much you've learnt about yourself through recovery. I personally find looking at my ill pictures encouraging to me to keep putting on weight, as I am able to see how awful I looked, and hate it. Be aware of the bad times to avoid romanticising the illness.

Chapter Nine

Back in the Real World

After being cocooned in my illness for several years, and then hidden away in the protective environment of the hospital, it was refreshing and exciting to come out into the real world, full of novelties and opportunities. On my first few visits home, I felt like a china doll, coming out and seeing the world through new eyes, yet fragile and secretly relieved that I could return to the safety bubble of the hospital.

Being from a family that thoroughly enjoyed their food, and often spent the whole evening sitting chatting around the dinner table, umming and ahhing over the delicious cuisine of the evening, and enjoying spending time together, I actually looked forward to being permitted to join them at mealtimes, despite having developed a dislike of eating in front of people.

I'm feeling optimistic about eating with my parents, it will be nice for them to see that I'm capable of eating as much as they are, and nice for me to sit with people who aren't terrified of the plate in front of them!

It was wonderful to eat with the parents; Mum gave me a hug and said she was so glad that I was getting better.

It's been so long since I've seen my house; the kitchen seems darker as if it's all been varnished, and the bushes in the garden have begun to overgrow on to the path. I had a lovely candle-lit bubble bath, finally not having to sit on my hands to protect my bones from the hard plastic tub! Then climbed into bed with Mum and we chatted for ages. Dad said after that it was so nice to hear me upstairs, much more alive than when I left for hospital the first day. I snuggled into my clean, freshly-made bed. My bed! It's been so long since anyone's slept in it!

I arrived back at hospital at about 9pm, where everyone made a huge fuss of my hair and congratulated me on my A level results. I felt like the centre of attention for positive reasons, that people weren't only paying me attention because I was ill.

My day away made me so appreciative of little things, as small as being able to choose and enjoy all my 'naughty foods', do things that the old 'Ali' did like shopping and seeing friends. But I'm scared that this novelty only makes life seem exciting because I know I can't have it that often, and when I'm back for good, and the novelty wears off, what will happen then? I felt safe knowing that I'd be back in the security net of the hospital not long after my venture out into the big, scary world.

I attended The Priory for three months, which involved both in-patient and day-patient care, the latter helping me to adjust to the difficulties of living in the real world as a recoverer, yet still having the security of the safe, hospital environment to come back to. As my days at The Priory decreased, I often went through spells where I was sucked back into the illness, torn between guilt of eating, and guilt of losing weight.

As my social time out in the world increased, people began to notice the slow but sure changes in me, and even now when I meet someone who hasn't seen me since I was at my worst, they comment on how 'I'm Ali again'. There is no greater compliment than being told I've 'got my spark back'.

Things that have helped in recovery

- Seeing the illness as a bully that has deprived me of everything, manipulated me. It constantly threatens me and relishes the fact that everyone around me is helpless, feeding off my vulnerability. It fills me with self-hatred and anger which only hurts me when I let it eat me up inside. Don't let the bully come between you and your life; talking and sharing difficult experiences helps so much.

- Positive mindset that keeps you strong, making the fight more bearable. But don't beat yourself up when times get hard; mistakes are only lessons and recovery is 'three steps forward, two steps back'. There is no consistency with the illness and it flares up without warning. It catches you off guard at your weakest moments, but complying with it only makes it stronger.

- I've eaten so many of the foods I thought I could never enjoy without guilt, and I've done the scary deed of putting on weight; both of which have only proved to be beneficial in helping the real me come back. Support from professionals and other sufferers who understand and have felt my pain. I don't feel like such a freak when I know I'm understood, and my illness is genuine and shared. This isn't seen as a plea for attention, or a diet gone out of control. I don't feel judged, and honesty with both myself and others is vital for recovery; lying only strengthens the illness.

- This journey helped me to see how strong I am, and I don't have to restrict food/over-exercise to prove my determination, willpower and control. I'm capable, and have a long life ahead of me in which the opportunity to discover, love and learn is there. I think optimistically and excitedly of the future which doesn't necessarily need to be mapped out. Life without anorexia will be more satisfying than a life which I have no control over.
- Avoid body checking, weighing and comparing, remembering how the anorexia distorts your mind's eye. Accept that you feel bad and stay with it; the focus and negative self images do gradually diminish. Distraction helps; remember that a balanced, nutritious diet is essential for a healthy mindset, not just weight or body.

Now

With my physical appearance improved and my discovery of my strength, we decided that this would be a good opportunity to visit my relatives in Chile for two months.

I knew how risky a trip away was to my recovery, and that such a huge change was a common cause of relapse for many newly-recovered anorexics. I was terrified that with the change of culture, people, temperature and food, my anorexia would find an avalanche of excuses for me to not eat, and would swoop back in, leaving me in the dark place that I'd fought so hard to get away from.

However, after often being told that recovery is about taking risks, I decided to go, and I don't think that I've ever made such a brave and positive decision; for my mental recovery, it was the best thing I'd ever done.

Despite losing weight, I gained so much mentally that I felt I was becoming a stronger, more developed person that could see the truly important things of life and was ready to get on with her life, without letting an illness live it for her. I saw how it had taken away the little things that mattered to me, like developing relationships with my family. I saw how loved I was, and how much pain those around me had suffered whilst I was caught up in my own little twisted world. I was able to become slightly less frantic by accepting the fact that I didn't need to be constantly on the go, and it was acceptable to just relax.

I came back refreshed and motivated to continue recovery in every aspect in order to blossom into the person that I wanted to be, and had eventually come to like. On New Year's Eve 2007, I raised my glass to my family and said, 'My New Year's resolution; no more rules!'

After a gap year in which I was able to travel, relax without the pressures of study, and learn to use the techniques of recovery in everyday life, I decided that I was ready to take the next step in life by taking up the place that I had deferred in Cardiff University to study English Language and Literature. Although I was warned of how easy it is for the illness to take control in such an independent lifestyle, I was determined to try and take the risk. I wasn't prepared to let the illness control me by holding me back for yet another year, and felt ready for mental stimualtion that I had missed during my year off.

The run up to uni was quite nerve-racking, yet on arrival, I was pleased to meet my flatmates; a friendly group of gap year students who were all as nervous and excited as each other about the step forward that they were taking in life. At first I wanted to ignore the fact that I had been so ill, yet the friendliness and openness of my flatmates allowed me to talk about my terrible experience, which was a huge weight off my shoulders. It's not always easy, and life is a series of ups and downs. But what I've realized since being in university is that everyone has their trials, and their own ways of coping. I felt that for so long I had taken on the identity of the illness, and during that time I had lost sight of who *I* was, but in university, I am able to try out new things, meet new people, and live a more independent lifestyle.

Anorexia is such a dominating illness that I'm still aware that it is there. However, it's the actions that you take that keep it alive. I refuse to let it dominate my life, making sure that I visit a nurse to monitor my weight each week, and to ensure that the numbers on the scales are not being controlled by my illness. It's very easy to skip a meal, or allow the illness to slip back into control, but I have made the decision that I want to live my life, and not allow this destructive illness to control me, destroy me, and eventually kill me.

Things are always up and down, and just because I feel stronger one week, it doesn't mean from then on I'll be able to cope. When times are hard, I just think of how I've had enough of the illness taking control, and deciding how each day will be.

Sometimes I get anxious and obsessive over meals, needing to plan out exactly what I'm having, and any changes throwing me into panic. But these times are becoming less frequent, and lasting for shorter periods.

Being able to sit with my family and enjoy a meal, without focusing on the food aspect but just enjoying the company and atmosphere, or being able to go out for a meal with friends and not having to excuse myself to run to the toilet in tears, makes the fight worth it.

I believe that through perseverance, determination and self-love, I can defeat the slowly diminishing voice that still echoes in my mind, and one day, it will be no more. Until then, I fight on to become the person I aspire to be. Living life, and loving every moment of it.

'When we live we are, but when we suffer we grow.'

I may never know the specific reason why I developed anorexia. I still wonder whether there will be one day in which it is all just a distant memory – but I believe that everything happens for a reason, and my anorexia was simply a chance for me to develop and grow.

I now respect the girl that I am, look forward to the future and acknowledge the fact that life is not a string of happy, Hollywood film events of perfection; hard times are often the times in which we learn most about ourselves. I now know I'm strong, and deep down no matter how hard I find the struggle against my demon, it is always worth every inch of the fight from being where I know the anorexia would take me.

I've come to learn that everyone makes mistakes, everyone has flaws and I don't need to hide behind a perfect mask to be accepted by others. Some people will like me, others won't, but they can decide that by the person that I am rather than the person I'm pretending to be, or have become by obeying an illness.

I won't pretend that everyday is not a struggle; sometimes I feel like I'm right back to where I was a few months ago; that all the hard times and struggles I've been through to get me to the top have been some useless dream. I sometimes think, 'What's the point in fighting so hard when it's so easy to lose it again?'

But then I remember how much I suffered when I gave myself up to the illness; lost in a miserable torrent of self hate, disgust and emptiness, hating where I was but being too weak to take myself anywhere else. Hospitalization gave me the physical strength to know that I could win this battle mentally, and although how good you look doesn't necessarily match how good you feel, I never want to go back to rock bottom.

Chapter Ten

Fighting for Treatment

Having no help in Wales apart from weekly visits to my psychiatrist, which didn't seem to be doing me any good, it was a struggle to get funding and hospital help.

I don't remember much from when I was at my rock bottom; I forget any social occasions with my friends, or any emotion. I was just an empty shell, and was so lucky to get the hospitalization I needed, in the nick of time. I never wanted to go to hospital, even when there I didn't want to stay – but who does?!

The fact was that I needed help desperately, and if I hadn't received hospital care when I did, I wouldn't be alive today.

The amount of funding I was given would be decided every six weeks depending on my progress and need to stay in hospital, in a CPA [Care Programme Approach] meeting involving my doctors, my home psychiatrist and myself. I found these meetings very difficult as despite being desperate to escape the hospital, I knew that for my own good, it would be best to stay.

Although I've only been here three weeks, I dread the thought of six weeks' more funding. However, to think of going back to a life totally consumed by anorexia makes me feel that that life is never worth going back to. Not in a suicidal way, but in the viewpoint that staying here will be beneficial in the long run.

I had my CPA where I got accused of being the perfectionist who hid her feelings, and they asked for twelve weeks' day care, if not four more weeks' inpatient; not a happy bunny about that! I think I'd probably have to discharge myself if it came to that!

Decisions on funding were always very last minute, and caused me a lot of stress and confusion as to whether I could go back home. The excitement of going home back to my friends, family, bed, home was often dashed at the last minute with the heart-breaking news that it was decided I must stay longer.

I have been trying to chase up the results of my funding, as I was meant to find out yesterday, but they still haven't gotten back to me. I need to know whether I'm leaving on Monday, or if I've got another six weeks of living here!

One of the girls who I have been very close to was told that she was to pack up her things and leave in an hour as her funding had run out! I was so sad to see her go, she's not ready and I'm so worried that the whole time she's spent here will have been a waste of time. As it's the same funding committee that are funding me, I know that the possibility of it happening to me is there, and sometimes I feel like I desperately want to leave here but I know that I'm unready to face the illness alone. I'm so thankful to have this opportunity to get better with constant support.

I got the horrible news that I am staying in for more funding . . . noooo!!!

I should just get on with it, fight the anorexia and forget about feeling miserable. I'm starting to see how it might be for the best to stay in, even though I don't want to one bit, it's what I have to do.

After chatting to another in-patient, I realized it's not so bad to have to stay; what will come out of it is that I'll only have more assistance in getting better. I want to escape the anorexia, that's why I want to escape from here, but I realize at home that anorexia is much stronger and it would be so much more overwhelming there. Sometimes I want to give up because the struggle to get better seems worse than the struggle to be anorexic, but I must keep at it; at the end of the battle, it will be worth it and I will have my life back.

When it was decided that I could no longer be funded as an in-patient, and my care was reduced to being a day-patient, the doctor warned me that I wouldn't cope in the real world. However, this just made me more determined to prove to the doctors, and most of all myself, my capability to escape the clutches of my illness. After all, I didn't want to lose all the good efforts and achievements I had made as an in-patient.

I'm so relieved I'm a day patient. Currently my attitude is 'Get on with it; it's all good.' Just take each day as it comes and yes, it will hurt, but plough on through and more than likely what is on the other side is so much better than the anorexia. I'm so very happy and confident; I'm ready to stay strong.

* * *

Since my hospital treatment, I have involved myself in raising awareness for eating disorders, trying to emphasize the necessity for an in-patient unit in Wales to be provided for people of my own age.

I find it unacceptable that there is no sense of urgency in supporting sufferers, who are simply left helpless and neglected. An initiative to provide some care centres in Wales will not only help people to feel more able to discuss their problems, reducing stigma and creating a sense of support, but will prevent any further deaths of sufferers, through prolonged suffering driving them to suicide, or simply that their bodies are incapable of continuing fighting.

What I find particularly infuriating is the way that it is decided which sufferer is most in need of help – leaving it until the person is at a dangerously low weight allows the illness to develop and get a stronger grip on the sufferer. Would doctors refuse to treat a cancer patient until the tumour was externally apparent? Weight level is not a measure of how much mental suffering someone is going through, and allowing the illness to develop only makes it more difficult, therefore more costly, to remove.

Afterword

Everyone has a journey to travel in life, becoming stronger by getting through it.

Imagine being stranded in the middle of nowhere; it's cold, dark and you're completely alone, with no light or map to guide you. Terrified, you realize that anywhere is better than the place you currently are, and so decide to embark on your journey.

Sometimes the road is smooth and you notice certain advantages of moving on.

But at times, the road becomes steep and uneven; giving up or falling back seems so much easier and a lot more convenient.

It's easy to put yourself down on days when you get lost, or at times when you become fearful of what's to come and start to retreat to a more familiar place in the past.

Where the path divides, you have to make a choice and take a risk.

Where you are offered help, you learn to accept it from others.

Barriers get in your way, but it's how you deal with them that matters.

There is no miracle, no magic transport to get you to the desired destination overnight, and it's not always going to be enjoyable or easy.

Yet every little step leads you slightly onward.

Do you simply give up and stick to what seems to feel 'safe'? Or do you take a risk, and then achieve your ultimate goal? What is more rewarding, and which choice will lead to a future for you?

After months of struggling, often through hard, lonely times, you finally reach your destination.

And it is paradise.

I was lost and alone, didn't know who to be,
and felt like an outcast, unaccepted for me.
When I needed a friend; a voice to console,
I heard a small whisper: 'You're not on your own.
I've seen you around and you're needing a friend,
and I promise to be there right until the end.'
I jumped at the offer of close company,
but little did I realize quite how close it'd be.
I felt proud to decline food – it showed me my
*   strength*
to say no to the things I would want at great length.
I felt so in control and my confidence soared,

what with all of the exercise, I was never bored.
People said 'what willpower it takes to do this!'
but little did they know it came with a twist.
I was hungry and desperate to eat a good meal
but the voice would get louder and started to squeal:
'What the HELL are you doing, you fat, dirty BITCH?!
We've got you SO far, now you shovel down THIS?!
It doesn't make sense to delay your progress!'
But by this point, I only began to obsess
about every morsel that passed my lips
added shame and disgust to the top of my list.
Temptation's no match for this beast that's inside
that slowly consumed me – I had nowhere to hide.
It was eating me up, and rotting my soul –
If it were to continue, it'd swallow me whole.
My clothes wouldn't fit and my body was frail,
but no matter my state I couldn't possibly fail.
The anorexic voice that drowned out the lot
of my terrified family, begging me to stop,
who crept into my room in the dead of the night
to see if their daughter was still breathing all right.
People gasped at my bones that protruded my skin,
pointing with horror at 'the girl that's so thin!'
I was ashamed and afraid, so much internal pain,
I thought I would never become me again.
It was the worst nightmare I could possibly know

as even when I woke up, it was there in full flow.
At a rock bottom where I could have easily died
finally, hospital help had arrived!
It took away control of anorexia's ways
and slowly but surely I started to change.
My passion for life started to get on track,
I can't tell you how good it feels to be back!
With recovery started, I learnt to control
the anorexic voice, and listen to my own.
But I still live in terror of the voice I followed,
dragging me back to its world of sorrow.
So I'm sharing my story of horror and pain
to prevent this from happening to anyone again.
I can never repay those who supported me through
the hardest time of my life – all I say is

Thank you

Useful Contacts

The Priory
Phone: 0845 60 50 121
Email: enquiries@prioryhealthcare.com
Website: www.prioryhealthcare.com/eatingdisorders

Beat (Beating Eating Disorders)
BEAT Helpline: 0845 634 1414
Email: help@b-eat.co.uk

BEAT Youthline: 0845 634 7650
TXT: 07786 20 18 20
Email: fyp@b-eat.co.uk

Open Monday to Friday 4:30pm–8:30pm
Saturdays 1:00pm–4:30pm
Sunday – Closed
Bank Holidays 11:30am–2:30pm

Website: www.b-eat.co.uk

An online 1-2-1 service is available which allows people under 25 to chat with the youthline through the website. 1-2-1 is available 5:30pm–7:30pm on Mondays, Wednesdays and Thursdays.

Samaritans

Phone: 08457 90 90 90 (UK)
         1850 60 90 90 (Republic of Ireland)
         Open 24 hours

Childline

Phone: 0800 11 11
Open 24 hours

Useful Information

Five facts about eating disorders

1. Eating disorders can be beaten.
2. An eating disorder is serious.
3. An eating disorder is not a dieting craze.
4. An eating disorder is not attention seeking.
5. An eating disorder is an illness.

About beat

beat is the leading charity supporting people affected by eating disorders and campaigning on their behalf. We provide helplines for adults and young people, a national network of self-help groups and the most comprehensive website on eating disorders in Europe. We campaign, supporting young people like Ali to talk publicly about their experiences, promoting understanding and highlighting how services can be improved.

We know that eating disorders affect over 1.1 million people in the UK, people of all ages, from all backgrounds, both men and women. But too many people think that eating disorders are a fad or fashion, a lifestyle choice. They don't understand that eating disorders are a psychiatric condition which has a devastating effect on the sufferer, their carers, family and friends. That's why it is so important that people like Ali can tell their story: it's a message of hope and a manifesto for change. Ali and her family fought to get her the treatment she so desperately needed: nobody should have to fight like they did. That's why **beat** campaigns to improve services, to challenge stigma and to ensure that people know that, like Ali, you can **beat** your eating disorder.

*A royalty on sales of this book goes to support **beat***